WORLD WAR II

Sky Pony Press books may be purchased in bulk at special discounts for sales promotion, corporate gifts, fund-raising, or educational purposes. Special editions can also be created to specifications. For details, contact the Special Sales Department, Sky Pony Press, 307 West 36th Street, 11th Floor, New York, NY 10018 or info@skyhorsepublishing.com.

Visit our website at www.skyponypress.com.

10 9 8 7 6 5 4 3 2 1

Manufactured in China, March 2015
This product conforms to CPSIA 2008

Library of Congress Cataloging-in-Publication Data
Murray, Stuart, 1948-
World War II / Stuart A. P. Murray.
pages cm
Includes index.
Audience: Grade 4 to 6.
ISBN 978-1-63220-433-2 (hc : alk. paper) -- ISBN 978-1-63220-818-7 (ebook)
1. World War, 1939-1945--Juvenile literature. I. Title.
D743.7.M87 2015
940.53--dc23
2015007042

Cover design by Georgia Morrissey
Cover photo credit: Thinkstock

FACT ATLAS

WORLD WAR II

Step Into the Action and Behind Enemy Lines from Hitler's Rise to Japan's Surrender

Stuart A. P. Murray

Sky Pony Press
New York

Contents

The War to End All Wars

 In early November 1918, the Great War (1914–18) finally came to an end after four long years of slaughter and destruction. A generation of young men was almost wiped out, and much of Europe lay in ruins.

This enormous struggle among the world's strongest powers involved 60 million soldiers, sailors, and airmen from dozens of countries. It cost more than 40 million casualties, including 20 million military and civilian dead. The conflict was fueled by past rivalries—some nations had fought each other for centuries.

On one side of the conflict were the Allies—the United Kingdom, France, Russia, Italy, and the United States. On the other side were the Central Powers—Germany, Austria-Hungary, and the Ottoman Empire. The war ended with complete victory for the Allies and utter defeat for the Central Powers.

The Great War was also known as "The War to End All Wars." It was supposed to be the beginning of lasting peace everywhere on Earth. No nation wanted another such disaster. In the hope of maintaining world peace, fifty-eight nations joined together in 1919 to form the League of Nations. The League's purpose was to preserve peace and solve international disputes.

DID YOU KNOW?

US forces were not engaged in major fighting until a few months before World War I ended. Still, US losses were heavy. In just the last six weeks of war, the United States suffered 117,000 casualties. By war's end, more than 50,000 had died and 205,000 were wounded—a terrible and unexpected loss to the country.

The end of World War I saw significant changes in Europe. Territorial lines were redrawn, with Germany losing significant land back to Poland and France.

Europe Before and After World War I
● city

BEFORE

ATLANTIC OCEAN

North Sea

SWEDEN

DENMARK ● Copenhagen

UNITED KINGDOM

RUSSIAN EMPIRE

● Minsk

NETHERLANDS ● Hamburg

London ● ● Amsterdam ● Berlin Warsaw

Brussels

BELGIUM GERMAN EMPIRE Poland

Paris ● Prague ● ● Cracow

FRANCE Vienna ●

SWITZERLAND ● Budapest

AUSTRO-HUNGARIAN

EMPIRE ROMANIA

ITALY Sarajevo ● Belgrade ● Bucharest ●

Rome ● SERBIA BULGARIA

Lisbon ● Madrid Sofia ●

PORTUGAL SPAIN ALBANIA

MONTENEGRO GREECE

Mediterranean Sea

AFTER

ATLANTIC OCEAN

North Sea

SWEDEN ESTONIA

LATVIA

DENMARK ● Copenhagen LITHUANIA

UNITED KINGDOM

● Kaunas

NETHERLANDS Hamburg USSR

London ● ● Amsterdam ● Berlin Warsaw

Brussels

BELGIUM GERMANY POLAND

Paris ● Prague ● ● Cracow

CZECHOSLOVAKIA

FRANCE Vienna ● ● Budapest

SWITZ. AUSTRIA HUNGARY ROMANIA

Belgrade ● ● Bucharest

Lisbon ● Madrid ITALY YUGOSLAVIA BULGARIA

Rome ● Sofia ●

PORTUGAL SPAIN ALBANIA

Mediterranean Sea GREECE

But Germany was determined to rise again. New German leaders came to power and began to rebuild the military, stronger than ever, and prepared to reclaim lost territory. Within twenty years, the Great War would have a new name: World War I.

In 1939, World War II would explode into an even mightier struggle, with greater destruction and loss of life. There would not, as yet, be a war to end all wars.

Above: Drafted by representatives from allied countries, the Treaty of Versailles peace document was signed in France on June 28, 1919, officially bringing World War I to an end.

DID YOU KNOW?

World War I came to an end on the 11th hour of the 11th day of the 11th month: 11 a.m. on November 11, 1918. This marked the end of fighting, an armistice. This gave the name to Armistice Day, an annual holiday in many nations honoring war veterans. November 11 is now known in the United Kingdom and Canada as Remembrance Day and in the United States as Veterans Day.

The *New York Times* headline tells the story of the end of World War I.

World War I battles were often fought in trenches, with combatants so close to one another that they could see the enemy's faces. Here, German soldiers prepare to defend their positions as they await a French attack.

CONQUER AND DIVIDE

WHEN PEACE TERMS were made in 1919, the victors tried to make sure the losers would remain weak. The defeated Central Powers were broken up into smaller states. Out of the ashes of war new nations appeared in Europe, including Czechoslovakia, Yugoslavia, Poland, Latvia, Lithuania, Estonia, and Finland. During the war, the Communist revolution threw down the Russian tsar (emperor) and established the Union of Soviet Socialist Republics (USSR).

The Rise of Hitler and Nazism

In the early 1920s, two political ideologies were winning followers around the world and especially in Europe. These were communism and fascism.

Communists wanted a society in which everyone was equal. Ideally, each person would work according to their abilities and be paid according to their needs.

Fascism allowed more free enterprise than communism, but neither theory allowed democracy. Both gave government absolute control over the people. As fascist and communist political parties gained popularity in Germany, they became bitter enemies.

A new political organization with fascist policies—the National Socialist German Workers Party—was led by former soldier Adolf Hitler (1889–1945). Its members were often called "Nazis." Hitler's party accused communists (some of

Born in Austria in 1889, Adolf Hitler served as a soldier in World War I. He later blamed Germany's loss on various groups including Jews and communists. He did not officially become a German citizen until 1932.

HITLER BECOMES *DER FUEHRER*

IN JANUARY 1933, Adolf Hitler was appointed chancellor, the supreme authority of Germany's *Reich* (empire). He immediately banned the Communist Party. That February, fire badly damaged the Reichstag, the main government building in Berlin. Hitler received emergency powers that made him dictator, a totalitarian ruler. He immediately ordered the arrest of 4,000 communists, accusing them of responsibility for the fire. (This was a lie.)

Hitler then declared the dawn of a new German empire—the Third Reich. He ended democracy and imprisoned thousands more opponents. Concentration camps held political prisoners who had no right to trial or to lawyers. Nazism had Germany in an iron grip, and Hitler began to rearm.

After the Reichstag fire in 1933, the building was too damaged to use for government business.

whom were Jewish) of causing defeat in World War I. Hitler falsely claimed that the military had been betrayed by Jews and communists who wanted peace rather than victory.

After the war, Germany was forced to pay hundreds of millions of dollars to the Allies, as reparations. These funds repaid the victors for wartime losses, but Germany itself was left in poverty. Times became so hard that many German citizens were starving. As a result, the population wanted to defy the peace terms, rearm, and reclaim all territory lost by the war.

In 1923, Hitler led a rebellion trying to overthrow the government. He failed and was imprisoned for thirteen months. But he had made a name for himself.

Once free, he found many supporters. Among them were generals and admirals determined to take control of the government. With these officers came the German military and also former servicemen. These became troops who fought for the Nazis, viciously attacking political opponents.

Most opposition was crushed by 1933, and the officers put Hitler in charge of the government as *Der Fuehrer*, "the leader."

DID YOU KNOW?

Members of Hitler's party did not usually call themselves "Nazis," which opponents often used as an insult. Instead, party members used the term *National Socialists.* After Adolf Hitler took power in 1933, the term *Nazi* almost disappeared from use in Germany.

Above: As a result of the Reichstag fire, Hitler made most of his inflammatory speeches at a former opera house near the Reichstag building.

Above: In 1914, this German 50 million mark was worth almost 12 million American dollars. Nine years later it was worth practically nothing.

Right: The depression caused by World War I hit Germany very hard, leaving many of its citizens poor, hungry, and desperate.

Dictator Domination

Germany was not the world's only totalitarian nation in the 1930s. Fascist and communist dictators ruled several countries or parts of countries.

The most influential dictator of this time was Italy's Benito Mussolini, known as *Il Duce*, which means "the leader" in Italian. After World War I, Mussolini founded the militaristic Italian League of Combat. Like Hitler, Mussolini created a one-party police state, with no opposition permitted. He planned a new Roman empire around the Mediterranean and in Africa. By 1936, Italian troops controlled Libya in North Africa and Ethiopia in eastern Africa. Mussolini and Hitler also supported Spanish fascists, led by General Francisco Franco (1892–1975), fighting their own republic's elected government.

Meanwhile, on the other side of the globe, Japan was the strongest military power, with one of the world's largest navies. Its government was under the dictatorship of military leaders. Since

DID YOU KNOW?

The Spanish Civil War was the testing ground for the world's newest weaponry. German, Italian, and Russian equipment was used by the opposing forces, including modern dive-bombers that for the first time were intended to terrorize civilian populations.

A group of Italian-made dive-bomber airplanes drop their payload in a raid during the Spanish Civil War. This particular group of planes belonged to the Spanish Nationalist forces that were supported by Hitler and Mussolini.

General Chiang Kai-shek served as leader of the Chinese national government throughout World War II. He opposed the Japanese, as well as communists in his own country.

1931, Japanese forces had occupied parts of China and were building the Greater Japanese Empire in East Asia and the Pacific. Although Japan's young emperor, Hirohito (1901–89), was believed to have divine origins, he had little real influence over the military.

Two major Chinese forces were opposing Japanese plans on the Asian mainland: the nationalists, led by General Chiang Kai-shek (1887–1975), and the communists, led by Mao Zedong (1893–1976). Chinese nationalists and communists sometimes joined forces to fight the Japanese, but they often fought one another, too.

The most powerful communist dictator at the time was Joseph Stalin (1879–1953), leader of the USSR. By the mid-1930s, Stalin had imprisoned or executed millions of accused enemies. He had more blood on his hands than even the ruthless Adolf Hitler.

ATLANTIC
OCEAN

UNITED
KINGDOM

GERMANY POLAND

FRANCE **E U R O P E**

ITALY

SPAIN

A F R I C A

USSR

A S I A

JAPAN

PACIFIC
OCEAN

CHINA

INDIA

Dictators and Dominions, 1930s

	Stalin		Mussolini
	Hitler		Japan

Fascist dictator Benito Mussolini planned
to turn Italy into an imperial power.

STALIN AND HITLER

LIKE GERMANY, Soviet Russia (as the USSR was
known) was eager to regain territory lost after
World War I. Poland and the Baltic states of Latvia,
Lithuania, and Estonia had been carved out of
former Russian territory.

Stalin looked westward and saw Nazi Germany
growing in strength. Both he and Hitler wanted
to take over lands between their countries. Each
realized this might one day mean war between
them, but for now they remained at peace. First
they wanted to know if their ambitions for conquest
would be opposed by the democracies: the United
Kingdom, France, and the United States.

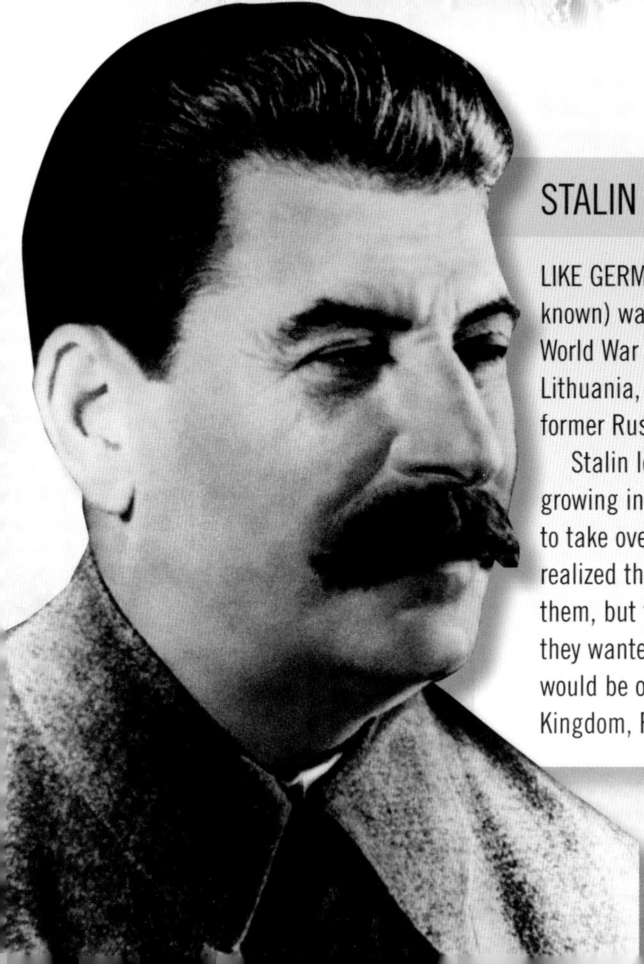

Though every bit as ruthless as
Adolf Hitler, Joseph Stalin's wartime
atrocities are often overlooked.

11

The Last Hope for Peace

United States president Franklin Delano Roosevelt came into office in 1933, just as Hitler took power in Germany. At first, Roosevelt concentrated on trying to bring the nation out of a deep economic depression, but he was also aware of the growing threat of Europe's dictators. Still, there was little he could do to stop Congress from passing the 1935 Neutrality Act. This act prevented the United States from shipping arms to any nation at war.

In 1936, Germany and Italy established the Rome-Berlin "axis," an alliance that was a danger to peace in Europe. In this same year, Hitler sent troops into the Rhineland, a German region next to France. This was a direct violation of the Versailles peace treaty. Still, France and the United Kingdom did nothing to stop Hitler's defiant move.

In the Pacific, Japanese sea and air power grew, posing a threat to American territories, such as the Philippine Islands and Hawaii. When full-scale war broke out between Japan and China in 1937, Americans aligned themselves with the Chinese.

In March 1938, Germany united with Austria, declaring it to be part of a greater German homeland. The democracies did nothing about it, hoping to maintain peace. But Hitler was not finished. In March 1939, he seized most of Czechoslovakia, without firing a shot. There was worldwide shock in August when the Nazis and Soviets signed a pact, each country promising not to attack the other. The British and French now made treaties, pledging to defend Poland.

On September 1, more than one million German soldiers invaded Poland. This time, the British and French declared war on Germany. World War II had begun.

Franklin Delano Roosevelt, the 32nd president of the United States. FDR shepherded the United States through the Great Depression while also keeping a watchful eye on the developments in Europe and the Pacific.

UNITED STATES

ATLANTIC OCEAN

Populations of Major World War II Combatants (in millions)

ALLIES	AXIS
China: 517.5	Japan: 71.4
Soviet Union: 168.5	Germany: 69.6
United States: 131	Italy: 44.4
United Kingdom: 47.7	
France: 41.7	
Poland: 34.8	

"PEACE IN OUR TIME"

IN SEPTEMBER 1938, British and French leaders met with Hitler and Mussolini in the German city of Munich to discuss Nazi demands. The subject was the northern Czech region of Sudetenland, which had a large German population and had been lost after World War I.

Hitler demanded the region be returned to Germany, and France and Britain soon agreed. No Czech officials were allowed at the negotiations, where the young nation was betrayed by the democracies.

According to British prime minister Neville Chamberlain, the Munich Agreement guaranteed "peace in our time." In fact, the agreement only assured the dictators that they would not bc stopped.

Upon his return to England, Prime Minister Neville Chamberlain waves a copy of the Munich Agreement as he addresses the assembled crowd.

UNITED KINGDOM

POLAND

GERMANY

FRANCE

E U R O P E

ITALY

USSR

A S I A

CHINA

JAPAN

PACIFIC OCEAN

A F R I C A

Blitzkrieg! and the Phony War

On September 1, 1939, Nazi Germany launched its invasion of Poland. The Polish military was strong in numbers but could not match the striking power of the German air force, called the *Luftwaffe*. Air attacks and the speed of German ground forces caused confusion in the Polish defenses.

These German tactics were known as "lightning war," or *blitzkrieg.* Europe was not accustomed to such fast-moving, hard-hitting attacks. German troops followed after the Luftwaffe strikes that weakened Polish defenses. Armored vehicles, called *panzers,* moved swiftly behind the Polish defenders and cut them off by the thousands.

By September 8, Nazi forces were close to Warsaw, the Polish capital. German air strikes on Warsaw killed more than 40,000 civilians. The Poles fought bravely, but on September 17, Soviet armies attacked them from the East. Warsaw fell on the 27th, and Poland's last fighters surrendered on October 5.

While the Soviets took over the defenseless Baltic states, Germany moved its forces westward to the border with France and the Low Countries (the Netherlands, Belgium, and Luxembourg). As the German expansion proceeded, the British and French did little in the way of offensive operations. They depended on their strong defenses, including France's Maginot Line, thought to be impossible to pierce. But Hitler had no intention of attacking the Maginot Line straight on. He would go around it and cut it off from the rest of the Allied forces.

The winter of 1939–40 saw almost no fighting along the frontier between Germany and the Allied nations of France and the Low Countries. There was little doubt that war would come, but the lack of fighting earned this period the name, "The Phony War."

This illustration of France's Maginot Line shows a much more elaborate defense system than what really existed. There were bunkers for officers and soldiers, but there were certainly no underground subways and other conveniences.

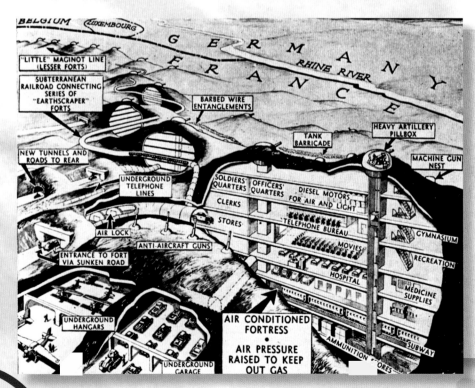

THE MAGINOT LINE

AFTER FIGHTING MUCH of World War I from trenches and machine-gun positions, the French built one of the world's finest defensive works, known as the Maginot Line. Five years of construction produced underground defenses that ran along France's border from Switzerland to the Low Countries.

The artillery shelters were built to resist bombing, and the walls were deep in the ground. Defenders were connected by an underground railway that moved troops and weapons quickly. The French expected to defeat any frontal assault on the Maginot Line.

These magnificent defenses were ultramodern but were designed for an old-fashioned war—not a blitzkrieg.

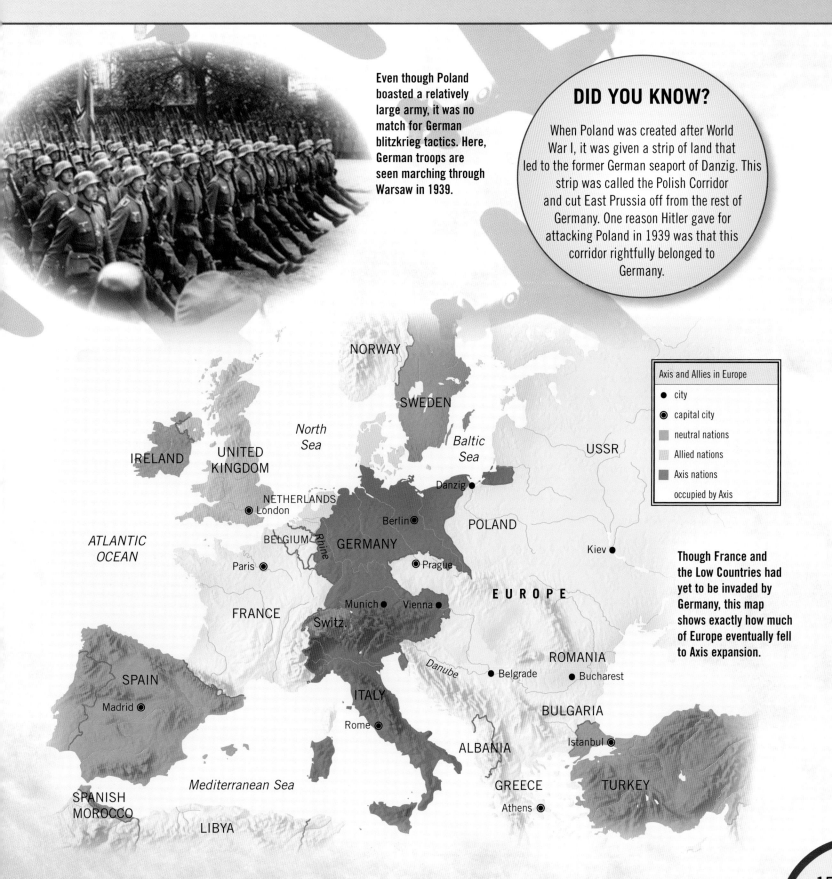

Even though Poland boasted a relatively large army, it was no match for German blitzkrieg tactics. Here, German troops are seen marching through Warsaw in 1939.

DID YOU KNOW?

When Poland was created after World War I, it was given a strip of land that led to the former German seaport of Danzig. This strip was called the Polish Corridor and cut East Prussia off from the rest of Germany. One reason Hitler gave for attacking Poland in 1939 was that this corridor rightfully belonged to Germany.

Axis and Allies in Europe

- • city
- ◉ capital city
- neutral nations
- Allied nations
- Axis nations
- occupied by Axis

Though France and the Low Countries had yet to be invaded by Germany, this map shows exactly how much of Europe eventually fell to Axis expansion.

NORWAY

SWEDEN

North Sea

Baltic Sea

USSR

IRELAND

UNITED KINGDOM

NETHERLANDS
◉ London

Danzig ◉

ATLANTIC OCEAN

BELGIUM

Rhine

GERMANY

Berlin ◉

POLAND

Paris ◉

Kiev •

◉ Prague

Munich • Vienna •

E U R O P E

FRANCE

Switz.

SPAIN

ROMANIA

Danube

• Belgrade

• Bucharest

Madrid ◉

ITALY

BULGARIA

Rome ◉

Istanbul ◉

ALBANIA

SPANISH MOROCCO

Mediterranean Sea

GREECE

TURKEY

LIBYA

Athens ◉

15

Defeat and Retreat

On mainland Europe, the armies prepared for combat through early spring 1940, but little happened. As German generals waited for everything to be in place before they attacked, the Allies hurried to train and equip their troops.

On April 9, German forces made their first moves. Nazi troops marched into Denmark, which surrendered quickly. The Germans also invaded Norway, but the Norwegians stubbornly defended their seaports—the objective of the Nazi invasion.

A few weeks later, the real ground war began. Thousands of German paratroopers dropped behind Dutch lines in the Netherlands. Waves of warplanes hit Holland's outnumbered military. Bombs rained down on the Dutch seaport of Rotterdam, destroying the center of the city. Holland's military surrendered, but the Dutch royal family fled to London to lead future resistance.

At the same time, a powerful German armored force pushed through the lightly defended Ardennes forest in Belgium. Following blitzkrieg methods, the panzers broke through and cut off the defenders from behind. The mighty Maginot Line was left useless. Nazi tanks and troop carriers surged across Holland and Belgium toward France, sweeping defenders aside.

British, French, and Belgian troops tried to counterattack, but the Germans had more warplanes and controlled the air. Allied troops and tanks were bombed and machine-gunned and found German panzers moving fast to surround them. By late May, many French troops and the British Expeditionary Force (BEF) were retreating toward the coast.

The troops at the coast were rescued from Dunkirk and taken to England, but France surrendered in June. Norway also fell to Hitler's forces, and only Britain was left to oppose Germany's Third Reich.

DID YOU KNOW?

On May 24, as Allied troops retreated to Dunkirk, Hitler ordered his panzers to halt. Historians wonder if Hitler hoped to make peace with the British. He delayed two days, allowing the "Miracle of Dunkirk" to occur.

German invasion of Low Countries and France

- ● city
- – – Allied lines
- Dunkirk evacuation route
- ◀ German attacks
- Ardennes forest

UNITED KINGDOM

London ●

Dover ●

Dunkirk ●

NETHERLANDS

BELGIUM

GERMANY

FRANCE

German troops methodically moved through the Netherlands (Holland, specifically) and Belgium as they made their way toward France. Though the Dunkirk escape spared many British and French troops, it wouldn't be long before the Nazis were in Paris.

THE DUNKIRK MIRACLE

BY MAY 26, MORE than 100,000 French and 200,000 British troops crammed into a pocket at Dunkirk on the French coast as German Messerschmitt warplanes screamed down to machine-gun and bomb them. The only escape for many was across the English Channel. With not enough warships or transport vessels to carry them away, they seemed doomed. Then, hundreds of British civilian and military craft went into action.

Tugboats, ferries, yachts, and naval vessels crossed and recrossed the choppy waters of the Channel, in one of history's most famous rescues. They saved more than 300,000 troops from the beaches and wharves, taking them to England so that they could fight again. Many considered the daring Dunkirk rescue a miracle.

The British military nicknamed the evacuation of Allied troops from Dunkirk Operation Dynamo. In addition to British naval vessels, hundreds of other private boats were used in the legendary escape.

Not everyone was lucky enough to escape Dunkirk. Here, British and French prisoners are marched up a hill in the French port town.

A German panzer tank

124

Bombs Over Britain

Hitler's ever-tightening grip on Western Europe divided France into two territories. The German military controlled the eastern coastal regions and the north, while a new French government ruled the rest of the country from the city of Vichy. The government of unoccupied France was called Vichy France and heavily influenced by the Nazis. The president of the Vichy government was the elderly war hero Marshal Henri Philippe Pétain.

Across the English Channel, the British rebuilt their military, especially fighter warplanes. In July, those fighters went into service when Hitler began a massive air campaign. At the same time, Hitler prepared for Operation Sea Lion, the invasion of Britain by sea.

Sea Lion's success depended on control of the skies over Britain, so the Germans sent their bombers to destroy Royal Air Force (RAF) bases. British Spitfire and Hurricane fighters attacked the bombers. The campaign, known as the "Battle of Britain," lasted through September. The Germans had far more aircraft—2,500—than the RAF's 1,200. In this same time, Luftwaffe bombers struck at British cities.

British civilians endured ferocious bombing, which they nicknamed "the Blitz." It lasted until spring 1941, killing more than 60,000 civilians. Hitler's attempt to defeat the RAF and break the British will to fight failed. The RAF won the Battle of Britain, and Hitler called off Operation Sea Lion.

German naval operations also attempted to choke off supplies coming to Britain. German "undersea boats," or U-boats, worked in stealth "wolf packs" to attack supply ships. The North Atlantic was the scene of massive destruction.

The courageous men and women back home, such as these British firefighters who helped put out blazes set off by German bombs, were just as important to the war effort as the military abroad.

With strategic air bases set up in the Netherlands, Belgium, and France, the Luftwaffe only had a short distance to fly in their bombing raids on Britain.

Battle of Britain, 1940
◆ German air bases
✎ German bombing targets

North Sea

Glasgow

Belfast

IRELAND

UNITED KINGDOM

Liverpool
Manchester
Hull

Birmingham
Coventry

Bristol

London

Atlantic Ocean

Plymouth

Portsmouth

English Channel

DENMARK

NETHERLANDS

Ghent
Brussels

BELGIUM

GERMANY

Beauvais
Deauville
Compiegne
St Cloud
Villacoublay

FRANCE

U-boat wolf packs almost won the Battle of the Atlantic, but British and Allied naval units soon matched these daring raiders. Eventually, the Allies developed tactics to fight off submarines and even pursue and attack them. Food and military supplies continued to flow over dangerous seas to Great Britain's shores from North America.

The Hawker Hurricane airplane was an RAF single-seat fighter that was instrumental in defeating the Germans in the Battle of Britain.

DID YOU KNOW?

During the Battle of Britain, the Nazis did not know that British air defenses had a new, secret weapon: radar. This electronic warning system spotted the approach of German aircraft and gave the RAF time to send up fighters to meet them. The Germans had lost the element of surprise.

Luftwaffe commander Herman Göring had been a highly decorated World War I flying ace.

A trio of curious British children sit among the ruins of their home, which was hit in a night bombing raid.

Following Neville Chamberlain's resignation, Winston Churchill became Britain's prime minister in spring 1940.

CHURCHILL AND GÖRING

TWO PRINCIPAL LEADERS during the Battle of Britain were British prime minister Winston Churchill (1874–1975) and Luftwaffe commander Herman Göring (1893–1946).

Churchill took charge of the British navy at the start of World War II. He was then appointed prime minister in 1940. Churchill's inspiring speeches and determination helped the British withstand the Blitz.

A fighter "ace" in World War I, Göring was an early member of Hitler's Nazi Party. He was later accused of poor leadership for failing to win the Battle of Britain.

War in the Mediterranean

The British fortified their island in 1940–41 and bombed Berlin in retaliation to Germany's attack on British cities. The Allied navies kept Hitler's surface-going warships mostly bottled up in European ports. Now, British leaders looked to fight on other fronts.

Millions of troops served in the forces of the British Commonwealth (formerly the British Empire). Canada, India, Australia, South Africa, and New Zealand had the Commonwealth's strongest militaries. Their forces combined with British units to challenge Germany and Italy. That challenge was made around the Mediterranean Sea, in the lands of Southern Europe and North Africa.

Key to this region was Egypt's Suez Canal, the shortest sea route from the Mediterranean to the Indian Ocean. The British had to protect that canal from capture by Axis forces. Italy had armies in Libya,

Formed by Benito Mussolini in 1919, the Black Shirts were the enforcers for his fascist agenda. Armed with his growing Black Shirt militia, Mussolini marched on Rome in 1922 and took control of the government by force.

DID YOU KNOW?

Although the United States was not a British ally in summer 1940, the two countries made the Destroyers for Bases Agreement that helped the British cause. In exchange for fifty older American destroyers, Britain gave America free leases to build naval bases in her colonial territories.

Ethiopia, and Somalia, and also controlled Albania. In September 1940, its forces invaded Egypt, pushing the British back and threatening the Suez Canal.

Encouraged by this success, Mussolini invaded Greece from Albania late in 1940. By December, the Greeks had thrown the Italians back, however, and had almost conquered Albania. To make matters worse for Mussolini, counterattacking Commonwealth troops under General Richard O'Connor defeated his forces in Egypt. In February 1941, when Allied forces captured more than 130,000 Italians, Hitler decided to aid Mussolini.

Late in February, German forces commanded by General Erwin Rommel rushed to North Africa. Other Nazi troops joined Italy's war against Greece, and British soldiers landed to support the Greeks. But it soon seemed that the Axis was winning everywhere.

That spring, Rommel drove the British back toward the Suez Canal. In late June, retreating British troops in Greece came under heavy Luftwaffe attack. They were forced to evacuate to the island of Crete. Without air support, the British navy in the surrounding waters suffered heavy losses to the Luftwaffe. Crete, too, was evacuated, and the Axis appeared almost unbeatable.

Hitler now planned an even more ambitious move: to attack the Soviet Union.

GREECE

TURKEY

Mediterranean Sea

TUNISIA

● Tripoli

● Tobruk

Benghazi ●

Suez Canal

ALGERIA

Nile

EGYPT

LIBYA

Driving Italians out of Egypt

● city

◄ British forces

— limit of British advance

— Italian lines

Italian retreat

Above: Knowing that they needed to protect access to the Suez Canal, British Commonwealth forces, under the leadership of General Richard O'Connor, drove the Italian army out of Egypt as far back as Tripoli in Libya.

WAR DATA

ONE OF THE FIRST British offensive strikes after France fell was to attack the Vichy warships to keep them from Axis hands. The Royal Navy and RAF bombed and bombarded French warships in Mediterranean and African ports.

A French squadron in Algeria was shattered, with more than 1,300 sailors killed and several warships sunk, damaged, or forced to run aground. British ruthlessness against their former ally proved the war would not soon end.

Nicknamed the Desert Fox, General Erwin Rommel was renowned for his military intelligence during his command of Germany's troops in North Africa. He later led German forces during the Allied invasion at Normandy.

Tyranny Rules

By early summer 1941, the Axis dictatorships controlled much of the world. The term "Axis" was first used the previous September when Germany, Italy, and Japan signed the Tripartite Pact, promising to aid one another.

Germany and Italy controlled much of Europe and North Africa, and Japan was moving against the Asian possessions of defeated France and the Netherlands. Japan's war in mainland China also continued.

The United States, led by President Roosevelt, watched with growing concern. With vulnerable American possessions in the Pacific, it seemed troubles might arise between the US and Japan. Although Roosevelt aided Britain militarily, he had promised to keep the United States out of the widening war. Tensions increased with Nazi Germany that spring when a U-boat sank an American merchant ship—the *Robin Moore*—in the Atlantic.

The course of the war suddenly changed on July 22, when Hitler launched a massive invasion of the Soviet Union. Stalin's forces were taken by surprise, and the Nazi blitzkrieg again smashed their enemy's defenses. The Soviets reeled under

Winston Churchill and Franklin Roosevelt sit aboard the HMS *Prince of Wales.* During their historic Atlantic Conference the two men outlined terms for a postwar peace.

Luftwaffe bombardment and swift panzer maneuvers. Although the Allies were grateful to have powerful Russia on their side, it seemed the Nazis soon would crush the Soviet armies.

The United States now was arming in case of attack by the Axis. In July, all American men over twenty-one were required to register for Selective Service, the draft. Although American bases in the Pacific were weakly protected, the growing US Navy was becoming powerful. Its main base was at Pearl Harbor, in Honolulu, Hawaii.

It was the Battle of the Atlantic, however, that seemed more likely to draw the United States into the war. A U-boat fired on a US destroyer, and Roosevelt ordered the navy to shoot at any vessel that attacked merchant ships. Roosevelt and Churchill met in Canada that summer to sign the Atlantic Charter, a declaration of human rights and principles.

The charter declared that people should have the right to choose their own government, and it called Nazi rule a "tyranny."

The course of World War II changed dramatically in summer 1941 when Hitler ordered his armies to invade Russia. Here, a German soldier throws a grenade at Soviet enemies while his comrade covers him with rifle fire.

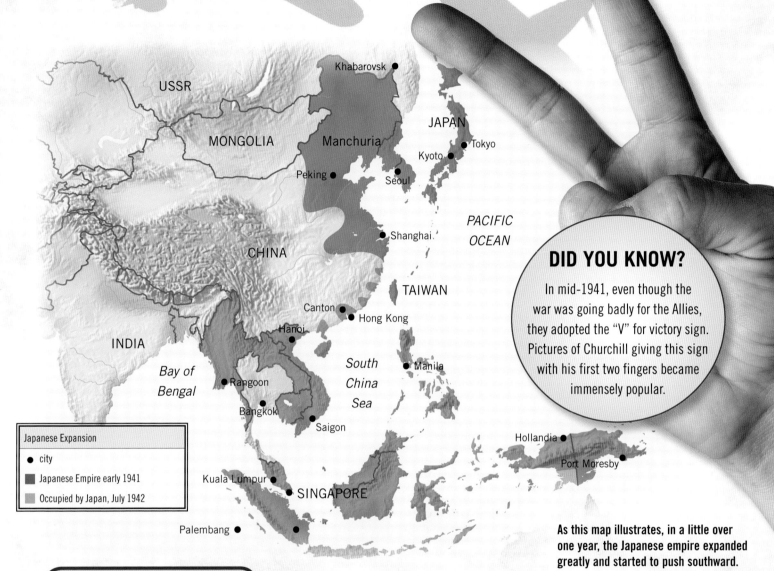

USSR

Khabarovsk

MONGOLIA

Manchuria

JAPAN

Peking

Kyoto

Seoul

Tokyo

CHINA

Shanghai

*PACIFIC
OCEAN*

TAIWAN

Canton

Hong Kong

Hanoi

INDIA

*South
China
Sea*

Manila

*Bay of
Bengal*

Rangoon

Bangkok

Saigon

Hollandia

Port Moresby

Japanese Expansion

● city

■ Japanese Empire early 1941

■ Occupied by Japan, July 1942

Kuala Lumpur

SINGAPORE

Palembang

DID YOU KNOW?

In mid-1941, even though the war was going badly for the Allies, they adopted the "V" for victory sign. Pictures of Churchill giving this sign with his first two fingers became immensely popular.

As this map illustrates, in a little over one year, the Japanese empire expanded greatly and started to push southward.

WAR DATA

IN MAY 1941, THE WORLD'S most powerful battleship—Nazi Germany's *Bismarck*—sailed into the North Atlantic. British warships moved to attack, but the *Bismarck's* guns sank the battle cruiser *Hood*, killing all but three of its 1,500 sailors.

More British warships hounded the *Bismarck*. Then, the growing advantage of warplanes over warships proved itself.

Planes taking off from an aircraft carrier attacked and badly damaged the *Bismarck* with torpedo bombs. Royal Navy guns soon did the rest, sinking the *Bismarck* with almost 2,000 crew members.

A scale model of the *Bismarck* as it looked in 1940. At the time of its launching in 1939, it was the largest and most impressive warship of its kind.

Rough Seas and Scorched Earth

 Military and political situations over the Atlantic and in Russia changed rapidly in fall 1941. Russian resistance to the blitzkrieg stiffened, and American relations with Germany grew ever worse.

Roosevelt continued to send supplies to Britain, carried by American and British merchant ships across the Atlantic. By now, the United States had a base in Iceland, with air and naval bases guarding the sea lanes against U-boat attack. The US Navy had orders to attack any German submarines entering into American waters. In mid-October, a U-boat torpedoed and damaged the destroyer USS *Kearney,* killing eleven sailors—the first American military casualties of the war. Later that month, the Germans torpedoed the destroyer USS *Reuben James.*

German soldiers lead captured Russian soldiers to prison camps.

It sank, with the loss of one hundred crew members. Further moving the United States into the conflict, Roosevelt approved the billion-dollar Lend-Lease agreement, sending military supplies to the Soviets as Stalin's forces struggled against the Nazi invaders. The cities of Moscow and Leningrad were under siege.

In a desperate attempt to slow the invasion, Stalin called for a "scorched earth" policy, destroying anything the Germans might be able to use. Soviet forces burned their own crops and bridges, blew up railroad tracks, and leveled towns.

The Germans captured or killed millions of Soviet troops. In many cases, they buried the dead in mass graves—as they had done with Polish officers. Jews, too, were rounded up and imprisoned. Many escaped eastward, but thousands were murdered.

By late autumn, mud slowed the German advance, and then came the bitter cold of the approaching Russian winter. Hitler ignored the advice of his generals who wanted to take Moscow. Instead, he ordered them to move southward to capture the oil fields of the Caucasus. His armies were stretched over a vast battlefront, with long supply lines that became targets for Soviet fighters.

By December, German troops were within 11 miles of Moscow, which seemed about to fall. Marshal Georgy Zhukov (1896–1974) led the Soviet defense of Leningrad. The German commander was General Heinz Guderian (1888–1954), leader in the blitzkrieg that defeated France. Then on December 6, Zhukov launched a massive counterattack, throwing Hitler's forces back on the defensive.

A statue of Russian war hero Marshal Zhukov riding atop his horse sits for all to see in front of the Historical State Museum in Moscow.

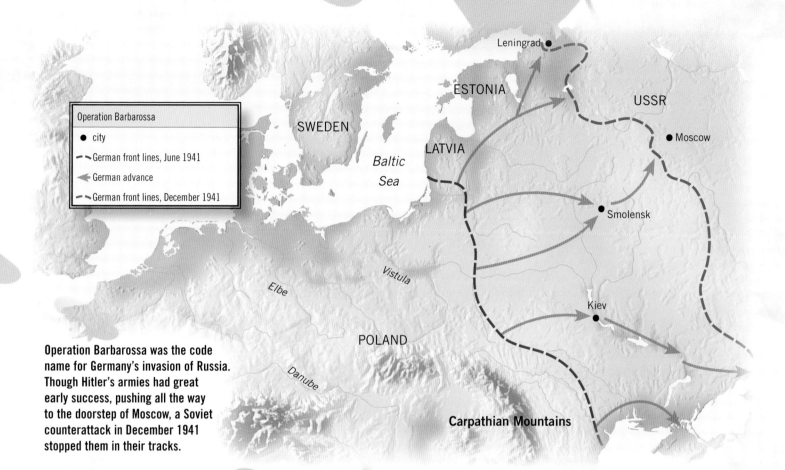

Operation Barbarossa was the code name for Germany's invasion of Russia. Though Hitler's armies had great early success, pushing all the way to the doorstep of Moscow, a Soviet counterattack in December 1941 stopped them in their tracks.

Operation Barbarossa
- ● city
- German front lines, June 1941
- German advance
- German front lines, December 1941

THE SIEGE OF LENINGRAD

A GREAT TEST OF HUMAN COURAGE and strength began in September 1941, when German forces attacked Leningrad. As the Soviet military battled on the ground and in the air, Leningrad's civilians labored with pick and shovel to dig trenches and build defensive positions.

Under heavy bombardment, suffering from lack of food and from cold weather, the defenders held out for more than two years. The siege was finally lifted by Soviet counterattacks in January 1944, but more than 830,000 civilians had died, most from starvation.

The brutal conditions during the siege of Leningrad caused hundreds of thousands to starve to death. Even finding something as simple as water (as pictured here) was an impossible task.

Surprise Attack!

 As the world followed military operations in Russia and in the North African desert, a Japanese war fleet secretly made their way across the Pacific toward Hawaii. The Japanese strike force included six aircraft carriers. The carrier's dive-bombers were armed with torpedoes designed to damage American ships docked in the shallow waters of Pearl Harbor.

Many American servicemen were still asleep in their barracks or on the ships when the first wave of warplanes struck early on Sunday morning, December 7. Honolulu, Hawaii, woke to the terrifying sounds of explosions, as bombs and torpedoes ripped open the vessels of the American fleet. A second wave of Japanese aircraft swept in an hour later. When the attack ended, eight US battleships and ten other warships were sunk or badly damaged. The battleships *Arizona* and *Oklahoma* were destroyed, and more than 2,400 Americans had died.

The USS *Arizona* is reduced to a smoldering wreck after the Japanese attack on Pearl Harbor. A memorial structure now spans the sunken ship, commemorating the 1,177 crewmen who lost their lives.

As fireboats struggle to put out flames aboard the USS *West Virginia*, smaller motor launches search the water for survivors. Though the ship sank, it was salvaged, rebuilt, and later participated in the Battle of Leyte Gulf in 1944.

The US Navy suffered a devastating blow by the surprise attack (the Japanese had not formally declared war beforehand). In reaction, Roosevelt declared December 7, 1941, "a date which will live in infamy." But the attack galvanized Americans. Immediately, the construction of a far more powerful US fleet began, with aircraft carriers a top priority. The United States now joined the Allies in a global war against the Axis.

Action to counter Japan's offensives would have to be swift. Right after Pearl Harbor, Japan set its sights on the Philippines, an important US possession.

Japanese bombs ripped through the forward machine-gun platform of the destroyer USS *Shaw*, setting off a large explosion. The ship somehow survived the attack and went on to see further action during the war.

DID YOU KNOW?

When war began between the United States and Japan, the American government ordered the arrest and detention of 110,000 residents with Japanese heritage. The government feared Japanese Americans would be more loyal to Japan than to the United States. In 1988, the US government formally apologized for this policy, because 62 percent of those interred were citizens whose rights were trampled on.

WAR DATA

AS 1942 OPENED, Japanese military power had great success. One crucial campaign turned the northern Philippine Islands into a major battleground.

Outnumbered American and Filipino defenders fought to keep from being surrounded and wiped out. They withdrew to the Bataan Peninsula, hoping for reinforcements that did not come. The United States did not have the military forces to help them.

The defenders were led by General Douglas MacArthur, who was ordered to escape to Australia and organize a wider campaign. The remaining forces fought on until May, and then surrendered. By now, Japan had won many of its Pacific objectives.

In California, US military personnel oversee a long line of "persons of Japanese heritage" as they arrive at an assembly center in Santa Anita on their way to so-called relocation centers, better known today as internment camps. The inset shows a young child sitting on a suitcase as she awaits transportation to a detainment facility. More than forty years later, the US government would apologize for its treatment of Japanese Americans during the war.

War in the Pacific

Top Japanese military leaders believed they could defeat the Allies if they captured and held important islands in the South Pacific. In this way, Allied naval forces would be prevented from shutting down sea lanes that brought vital oil supplies to Japan. Also, holding strong positions on these islands would make it difficult for the Americans—the strongest Allied military in the region—to attack them.

But the Japanese under-estimated the American will to fight, as well as the nation's determination to take revenge for the Pearl Harbor attack. One key advantage held by the Americans was that they had broken Japan's secret military code and knew what orders were being issued by radio to Japanese forces. This gave the element of surprise to the United States.

Although Japanese forces quickly occupied and fortified many islands, their troops were scattered far and wide. Support came from the Japanese navy, which shipped supplies and troops across thousands of miles of ocean. In early May 1942, Japanese naval movements in the southwest Pacific were challenged by the US Navy. A Japanese expedition landed on the Solomon Islands, intending to take New Guinea next, but it unexpectedly found an American carrier fleet bearing down.

The American and Japanese carrier fleets battled in the seas around the Solomon Islands. At first, it seemed that Japanese plans were going well, but the the United States scored an important victory at the Battle of the Coral Sea.

This was world's first major battle fought by aircraft only—most flying from carriers. The Americans lost the carrier *Lexington,* and the *Yorktown* was badly damaged. The Japanese lost several warships, including one carrier, with two others damaged. They had to abandon the expedition against New Guinea.

When another US carrier task force launched sixteen long-range bombers that struck Tokyo that spring, the Japanese people realized the war would be fought on their doorstep. The raid, led by General James H. Doolittle (1896–1993), inspired the Allies and proved that Japanese campaigns could be countered by American naval and air power.

Airforce Lt. Colonel James H. Doolittle (second from left) stands with members of his flight crew. After their daring raid on Tokyo, Doolittle was promoted to Brigadier General.

General James H. Doolittle was one of World War II's true heroes. President Roosevelt presented him with a citation that stated, in part, "With the apparent certainty of being forced to land in enemy territory or perish at sea, Colonel Doolittle personally led a squadron of Army bombers, manned by volunteer crews, in a highly destructive raid on the Japanese mainland."

TURNING POINT AT MIDWAY

IN JUNE 1942, a Japanese carrier force attacked the strategically located Midway Island, and American carriers counterattacked. The battle raged for three days, June 3–6, and again the Americans prevailed. Led by Admiral Chester W. Nimitz (1885–1966), US carriers sent out warplanes that sank all four Japanese carriers and a heavy cruiser. One US carrier, the *Yorktown,* was sunk.

The Japanese retreated, marking the turning point in the Pacific war, which continued for more than three years.

Black clouds of antiaircraft fire can be seen over the Pacific Ocean during the Battle of Midway. The three-day battle ended in an American victory.

The Solomon Islands
● Guadalcanal

PACIFIC
OCEAN

Solomon Islands

NEW GUINEA

Guadalcanal

Coral
Sea

AUSTRALIA

Some of the most bitter conflicts in the Pacific theater of war (which is the entire air, sea, and land area in which a war is conducted) took place on and around the Solomon Islands.

DID YOU KNOW?

On January 1, 1942, the Allies signed the Joint Declaration to fight the Axis until final victory was won. The official name of the twenty-six–country alliance became the United Nations. President Roosevelt is credited with coining the name.

Though damaged during the Battle of the Coral Sea, the USS *Yorktown* went on to fight in the Battle of Midway in June 1942. It was there, after numerous bombing attacks, the ship was abandoned on June 4 and torpedoed and sunk by a Japanese submarine three days later.

The World at War

As World War II reached its boiling point, so too did the effort to recruit new soldiers. In the United States, the popular image of Uncle Sam created by artist James Montgomery Flagg during World War I was updated and urged young men to "enlist now."

 In spring 1942, the war was raging around the globe. The new alliance between the United States and Great Britain sparked rapid growth in Allied military power. American industry fired up, millions of Americans were in training, and American-made war supplies filled merchant ships that crossed the dangerous Atlantic Ocean.

As German forces powered their way into Stalingrad, they were faced with a city as ravaged as the soldiers themselves.

I WANT YOU

for the U.S. ARMY ENLIST NOW

The Battle of the Atlantic raged more fiercely than ever. With the United States now in the war, U-boats attacked all along the eastern US coast. The US Navy was not yet prepared to protect convoys, and in the first months of 1942, more than a half million tons of shipping sank. Most U-boat attacks were within 300 miles of the coast, and nearly half of the US losses were oil tankers.

By now, the British had forced their way into several West Asian countries, taking control of Iraq, Syria, and Persia (present-day Iran). This oil-rich region was kept out of Axis hands—for now.

In North Africa's Western Desert, Rommel's army, the *Afrika Korps,* drove back the British and their Commonwealth allies. Matters were made even worse when U-boats sank major British warships in the Mediterranean.

In Asia and the Pacific, Japanese triumphs on land continued. British and Commonwealth forces surrendered

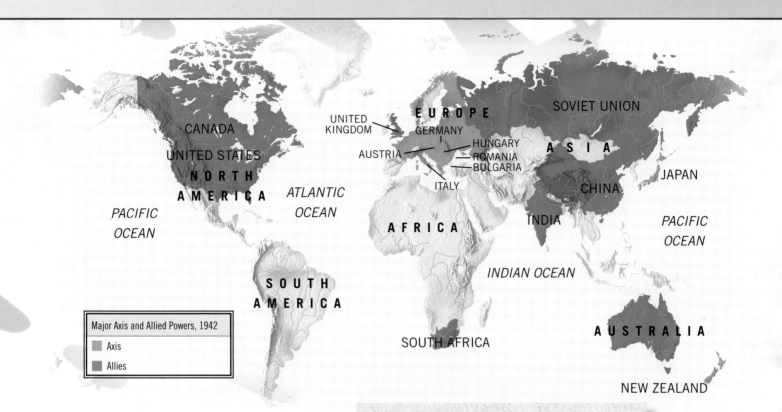

Major Axis and Allied Powers, 1942

Axis

Allies

Much of the world was divided into "Axis" and "Allies" during the long years of the war.

at Hong Kong and Singapore. India and Australia lived under worsening threat of invasion. China was too large for Japan to conquer easily, but the Japanese had a clear military advantage.

By summer, US industrial power began to make a difference. British forces in North Africa were being supplied with hundreds of American tanks. With their back to the Suez Canal, the British prepared to make a counterattack.

The Soviets also received American supplies and weapons. Despite enormous losses they held on against Nazi attacks. Then, Hitler ordered the capture of Stalingrad, on the Volga River. His most powerful forces battled their way to the city by late summer 1942 but at a great loss of troops.

Worldwide, the situation was desperate for the Allies, but the tide of war soon would turn.

FIGHTING FOR FREEDOM

EVEN THE MOST RUTHLESS Axis rule could not keep down the urge for freedom in occupied countries. Secret organizations appeared in many places, dedicated to resisting Axis control.

Resistance groups attacked enemy truck convoys in Yugoslavia, sent coded radio messages from Japanese-held islands, and helped Polish Jews escape Nazi persecution. The resistance often rescued airmen whose planes had been shot down over occupied territory. During the course of the war, resistance fighters rescued more than 33,000 downed fliers.

The occupiers executed suspected resistance members and took revenge on innocent civilians. Yet, the situation remained dangerous for Axis troops where armed civilian opposition was strong.

Wherever there was enemy occupation there were almost always resistance groups that were committed to fighting or sabotaging it by whatever means possible. Here a member of the French resistance and an American soldier fight side-by-side on a French street.

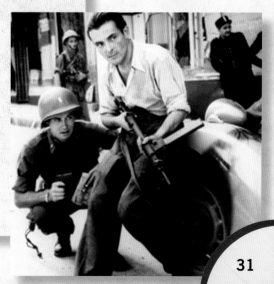

The Allies Strike Back

As American-led forces in the Pacific struggled to roll back Japanese invasions and naval operations, British-led forces fought the Germans and Italians in North Africa. In Russia, the Nazis and their allies fought the Soviets across thousands of miles of battlefront.

Allied air power grew stronger, bombing German cities, including Berlin. In the Atlantic, the Allies began to take a heavy toll on German U-boats.

In August, American marines landed on the Japanese-held islands of Guadalcanal and the Solomons. Some of the fiercest fighting of the war raged through steaming South Pacific jungles. This campaign continued until the following spring, ending with a Japanese defeat.

As Allied forces commanded by General Dwight D. Eisenhower landed in Vichy French North Africa, troops led by British General Bernard Montgomery were busy pushing Rommel's Afrika Korps right toward them.

STALINGRAD

THE BATTLE OF STALINGRAD was fought over seven months between the Soviets and the Germans, who also had troops from Romania, Italy, and Hungary.

The Soviets were led by Marshal Zhukov and General Vasily I. Chuikov (1900–82). The firepower and skill of the German Sixth Army met Soviet bravery and patriotism in the struggle for the city named after Joseph Stalin.

The harsh Russian winter was also on the Soviet side and crippled the invaders. By November, the Sixth Army was surrounded and completely destroyed by February. The Soviets losses totaled 500,000 killed; Axis losses were 147,000 killed and 91,000 captured.

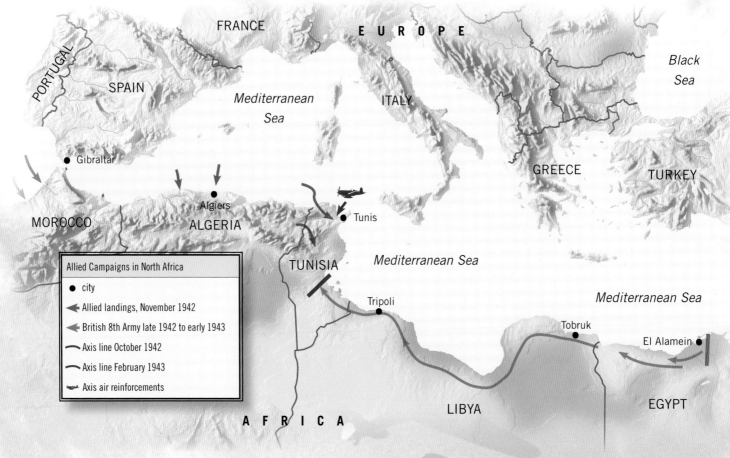

FRANCE

EUROPE

PORTUGAL

SPAIN

Mediterranean Sea

ITALY

Black Sea

Gibraltar

GREECE

TURKEY

MOROCCO

Algiers

ALGERIA

Tunis

TUNISIA

Mediterranean Sea

Tripoli

Mediterranean Sea

Tobruk

El Alamein

Allied Campaigns in North Africa

- ● city
- ◄ Allied landings, November 1942
- ◄ British 8th Army late 1942 to early 1943
- — Axis line October 1942
- — Axis line February 1943
- ◄ Axis air reinforcements

LIBYA

EGYPT

AFRICA

In this same period, British, Australian, New Zealand, Indian, and South African troops drove Rommel's Afrika Korps back across the Western Desert. Led by General Bernard Montgomery (1887–1976), the Allies used their greater firepower to defeat the Afrika Korps. After 60,000 casualties, Rommel's survivors retreated 1,750 miles to Tunisia. Meanwhile, Allied expeditions landed on the coast of North Africa and threatened Rommel from the west.

The Soviets, too, made the winter of 1942–43 a time of bitter defeat for the Axis, capturing an entire German army at Stalingrad.

American troops storm a beach near Algiers in November 1942. This landing was just a small part of the Allied invasion of North Africa code-named Operation Torch.

Matching wits against Erwin Rommel, General Bernard Montgomery's Allied forces used superior firepower to push the Afrika Korps across the desert and back to Tunisia.

WAR DATA

US GENERAL Dwight D. Eisenhower (1890–1969) led the British-American invasion of Vichy French North Africa in November 1942. Named Operation Torch, the plan called for troops to journey by sea from Britain and as far away as the United States.

Composed of mostly inexperienced troops, the expedition first battled Vichy French defenders. Most French did not want to fight the Allies, but each side suffered almost one thousand killed before the shooting stopped.

The expedition soon reached strong German-Italian defenses in Tunisia. What the Allied troops lacked in experience they made up for in courage and eagerness to fight.

General Dwight D. Eisenhower went by the nickname Ike. After the war, he went into politics, and in 1953 he became the 34th president of the United States.

War in the Atlantic

 The Battle of the Atlantic saw great Nazi successes in 1942. The first half of the year was costly to merchant shipping, because the US Navy had not yet learned to protect merchant ships.

American merchant ships did not follow the British practices of turning off running lights at night and following zigzag courses to confuse U-boats. Nor did American ships travel in convoys protected by warships.

The Nazis called this period a "happy time" for U-boats, which sank 609 vessels totaling 3.1 million tons. Most sinkings occurred close to North America. Only twenty-two U-boats were lost in these months. If the Allies could not ship troops and equipment from North America, then the war would be lost. In this struggle, the civilian seamen of the Allied merchant fleets were little-known heroes. Their toughness and courage brought thousands of ships safely to port in Great Britain. Many merchant seamen died.

By mid-1942, American antisubmarine forces had grown in numbers and in experience. U-boats were always in danger of discovery and attack. At the end of 1942, Germany was building U-boats with better technology. These newer submarines could patrol farther without refueling. The Battle of the Atlantic hung in the balance.

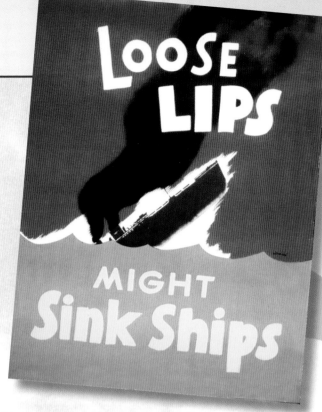

This poster, stating that LOOSE LIPS MIGHT SINK SHIPS applied to shipping information and convoy routes in the Atlantic. It was also a broad reminder to soldiers and civilians alike not to talk or write about any military information that could be useful to the enemy.

DID YOU KNOW?

Passenger ships carried millions of American and Canadian troops to Europe. The luxury liner *Queen Elizabeth* transported more than 150,000 troops during the war. The *Queen Mary* could carry 15-20,000 troops. These vessels usually traveled alone, counting on their superior speed to avoid U-boats.

During World War II the *Queen Mary* and other luxury liners were used to transport troops from North America to Europe.

OPERATION DRUMBEAT

THE U-BOAT campaign along the American coast was code-named Operation Drumbeat. A few U-boats sank hundreds of merchant ships in the first months of 1942, partly because American warships were escorting troop transports heading for Europe. No troop ship was lost during this time.

US shoreline communities did not turn off their lights at night—a blackout that could have concealed targets from enemy ships or planes. Therefore, U-boats could see ships leaving port, which were easy targets.

Later in 1942, the US Navy required merchant ships to travel in protected convoys, and U-boats withdrew from American waters.

WOLF PACKS

GERMAN U-BOATS often operated in groups called "wolf packs" to attack busy enemy convoy routes. Wolf packs totaling ten to fifteen U-boats usually struck convoys in two waves.

U-boats had to surface to recharge their air supplies, which they did at night to avoid being spotted and bombed by Allied aircraft. U-boats were most destructive in the sea lanes between Greenland and Iceland, where Allied air protection for convoys did not yet exist.

Once U-boats were discovered, explosives called depth charges were dropped to detonate near them. One highly effective explosive, the Hedgehog, was successful 25 percent of the time in sinking U-boats.

Men aboard the Coast Guard cutter *Spencer* watch as one of their depth charges explodes a German U-boat attempting to break up an Atlantic convoy.

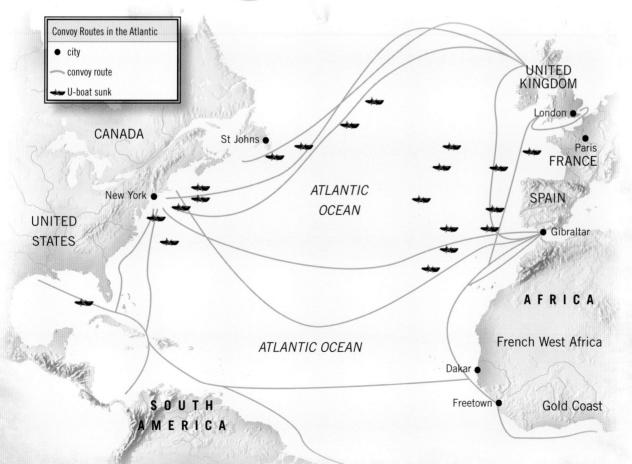

Convoy Routes in the Atlantic
- ● city
- — convoy route
- ⚓ U-boat sunk

CANADA

St Johns ●

New York ●

UNITED
STATES

ATLANTIC
OCEAN

UNITED
KINGDOM

London ●

Paris ●
FRANCE

SPAIN

Gibraltar ●

ATLANTIC OCEAN

AFRICA

French West Africa

Dakar ●

Freetown ●   Gold Coast

SOUTH
AMERICA

This map shows some of the Allied supply convoy routes used during the war as well as the primarily coastal areas where U-boats were spotted and destroyed.

The Fight for Guadalcanal

 Japan captured and fortified many islands around Southeast Asia and in the South Pacific. These bases were needed to control sea routes carrying oil tankers for the Japanese war effort. Japanese troops, ships, and warplanes were scattered widely across a vast region. As a result, they were left open to Allied offensives, such as that on Guadalcanal.

The battle for this island was one of the most important American campaigns of the war. It began in August 1942 with the landing of 19,000 US Marines. Japanese warplanes at first sank or drove off ships supporting the marines. This left the Americans without supplies or reinforcements or warplanes to protect them.

Japanese troops and supplies did land, while naval guns and aircraft pounded the marines. It took almost two months for the US Navy to break through the Japanese fleet and land thousands more marines. American army units also arrived, but the struggle raged until February 1943, when the Japanese were finally driven off Guadalcanal.

The fall of Guadalcanal, with its critical airfield, gave the Allies control of the strategic Coral Sea. It also offered a jumping-off point for new campaigns—with the ultimate objective being Japan itself.

This heavy machine gun was just one of many weapons used by the Japanese army during World War II. This particular gun was recovered by New Zealand soldiers and now resides in a museum in Auckland.

US Marines wade ashore on Lunga Beach on Guadalcanal. This scene would be repeated time and again in other Pacific island campaigns.

ISLAND-HOPPING

THE ALLIED VICTORY in the grueling Guadalcanal campaign opened the way for new operations against Japanese bases in spring 1943. The process of attacking base after base would earn the name "island-hopping."

Not only were Japanese bases on the many islands of the South Pacific attacked, but others were also "hopped." American forces allowed the thousands of troops on those islands to remain there, short of supplies and reinforcements. There was no reason to attack them, for that would have cost many Allied lives. Instead, they were left behind, eventually to surrender without a fight.

ATTU AND KISKA

TO SERVICEMEN AND WOMEN in the beautiful South Pacific, the names of tropical islands didn't mean sunny beaches but instead bloody battlefields: New Guinea, Papua, Rabaul, Tarawa, the Carolines, Gilberts, and Marianas. These islands had to be captured if Japan was to be defeated.

In the cool, misty waters of the Northern Pacific there was a different problem. It was an insult to American national pride that the Japanese had captured two Aleutian Islands, Attu and Kiska. As part of Alaska, they were American soil.

US forces attacked these islands during May and June 1943, meeting stiff resistance before retaking them.

Freezing temperatures and a relentless Japanese fighting force made the campaign to capture the island of Attu a particularly brutal one. American soldiers were forced to fight from trenches as Japanese forces took positions on higher ground and waited for the advance.

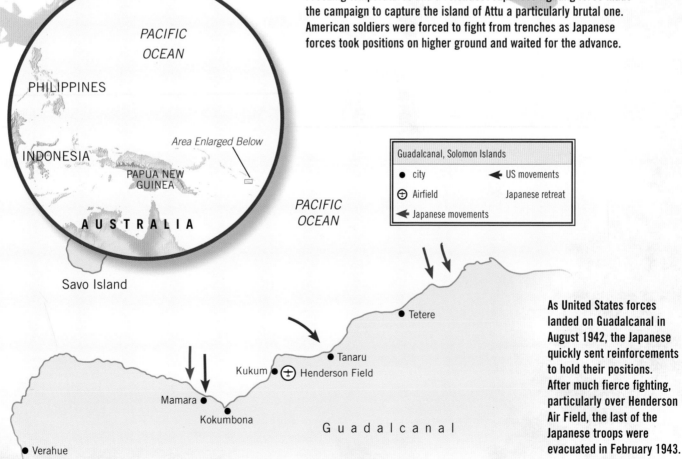

PACIFIC OCEAN

PHILIPPINES

INDONESIA

PAPUA NEW GUINEA

Area Enlarged Below

AUSTRALIA

Savo Island

PACIFIC OCEAN

Guadalcanal, Solomon Islands	
● city	◀ US movements
⊕ Airfield	Japanese retreat
◀ Japanese movements	

● Tetere

● Tanaru

Kukum ● ⊕ Henderson Field

Mamara ●

Kokumbona

Guadalcanal

● Verahue

As United States forces landed on Guadalcanal in August 1942, the Japanese quickly sent reinforcements to hold their positions. After much fierce fighting, particularly over Henderson Air Field, the last of the Japanese troops were evacuated in February 1943.

The Long Conflict in China

Chairman of the Communist Party of China, Mao Zedong (below) assembled a modest, yet committed, fighting force known as the People's Liberation Army. After World War II, Mao and his forces took control of China from the nationalists, led by Chiang Kai-shek.

Some historians date the beginning of World War II to the conflict between Japan and China that started in 1937. Even earlier Japanese aggression drove Chinese government forces out of key industrial areas, such as Manchuria. Japan then reestablished this province as Manchukuo, an independent state that they controlled. Its minerals and manufacturing were essential to Japan's military growth.

In mid-1937, Japan launched a full invasion of China, sending 300,000 well-trained troops against unprepared Chinese forces. General Chiang Kai-shek led Chinese nationalist forces, while another army was under Chinese communist control. During this Sino-Japanese War, these Chinese armies were sometimes allies and at other times fought against each other in civil war. The lightly equipped communists were led by Mao Zedong, whose People's Liberation Army often operated behind Japanese lines.

DID YOU KNOW?

In the 1930s, China and Nazi Germany had close relations, with Germany providing most of the Chinese government's military assistance. In 1938, Germany took Japan's side in the Sino-Japanese War, since Japan was clearly the more militarily powerful.

This map illustrates Japan's conquests in and around Asia prior to, and during, World War II.

Japanese Activities in Asia Through 1942

- city
- Japanese Empire in 1870
- acquisitions until 1932
- additional occupation by 1937
- additional occupation 1938
- additional occupation 1940
- additional occupation 1942

ASIA

JAPAN
Tokyo
Manchuria
KOREA
Peking
Seoul
Yellow River
CHINA
Nanking
PACIFIC OCEAN
Himalayan Mountains
Yangtze River
Hong Kong
Taiwan
BURMA
Hainan
FRENCH
PHILIPPINES
Manila
Rangoon
THAI-LAND
INDO-CHINA
Phnom Penh
Saigon
BRITISH MALAYA
INDONESIA

While Chinese Nationalist forces fought against Japanese invaders, they also tangled with Mao's communist army. Commenting on his two enemies, Chiang Kai-shek (left) said: "The Japanese are a disease of the skin; the communists are a disease of the heart."

WAR DATA

FOR YEARS, Japanese generals with massive armies waged war against China but had little real success. When the nationalists seemed defeated and made a truce, the communists would rise and fight. Then the nationalists would reorganize and return to the battle.

The Sino-Japanese War kept more than 1.5 million Japanese troops bogged down on the mainland. These soldiers—and their equipment, armor, and aircraft—were unavailable for the wider war in Southeast Asia and the Pacific. With the entry of the United States into the war in December 1941, Chiang Kai-shek declared war against Germany and the other Axis powers.

TIGERS AND TRUCKERS

BEFORE THE Sino-Japanese War, Chinese communists had received military aid from the Soviet Union in order to fight the nationalist government.

After the United States entered the war in 1942, Allied supplies and materials flowed in greater quantities to Chinese government forces. Most was transported over the Burma Road—a mountainous route between Burma and China—from British-held territory, but some came by airplane.

Since 1941, a squadron of American volunteer pilots had been employed by the Chinese nationalists. Known as Flying Tigers, they numbered about 250 pilots and support personnel. Their planes were P-40 Warhawks, famed for the sharks' teeth painted on their noses.

Major cities, such as Beijing, soon fell to the Japanese armies. By early 1943, the Japanese held the main seaports and most of northern and central China. The Japanese invaders even set up a puppet Chinese government, with Nanking as its capital.

The invaders considered the Chinese people a lesser race and committed many acts of mass slaughter against the civilian population.

The Curtiss P-40 Warhawk was an American single-seat fighter used in World War II. The shark's teeth on this plane were made famous by a volunteer group of former US military pilots known as the Flying Tigers who flew missions in defense of China.

The Jacky C.

Rescue from the Battlefield

 World War II was notable for the improved care of the wounded and sick. Yet, the most advanced technology would have been useless if not for the courageous army combat medic or navy corpsman. These individuals treated the wounded under fire, keeping them alive until they could be carried to a field hospital staffed with doctors. The same could be said for emergency volunteers who dug through rubble to find civilians buried during bombing raids.

As never before, the wounded of modern militaries could be rapidly airlifted—carried by plane—to well-equipped hospitals for intensive treatment of wounds. Advances in medical technology and swift medical attention drastically lowered the number of

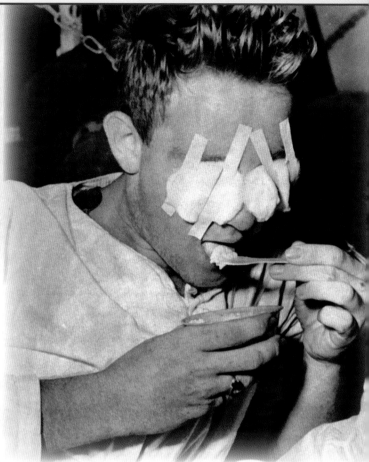

A wounded soldier, with injuries to his eyes, eats while recovering in the hospital.

military deaths resulting from wounds or illness. For example, in the American Civil War, the 364,000 Union army war deaths included 224,000 from illness or other causes. Of the 312,000 Americans who died in World War II, 292,000 were battle deaths, while only 20,000 were from other causes.

Germany lost 2.3 million killed in action, while 500,000 military personnel died from disease or accidents. Modern medical procedures saved many who otherwise would have died from wounds or illness.

US Army nurse grabs a shovel and pitches in as other workers put the finishing touches on the medical tent going up behind her.

PACIFIC OCEAN

Moreton Island

Centaur sunk X

Brisbane

North Stradbroke Island

Cairns

Area enlarged at left

Brisbane

AUSTRALIA

The Sinking of the *Centaur*
- ● city
- X site of sunken ship

Sydney

Melbourne

THE FLOATING HOSPITAL

WELL-EQUIPPED HOSPITAL ships were seagoing facilities for the more seriously wounded, who could not return to their combat units.

Hospital ships came equipped with doctors, nurses, emergency rooms, operating rooms, and the latest available technology. They could carry large numbers of wounded away from war zones to safe ports and permanent hospitals. Passenger liners, with their many cabins, were often put into service as hospital ships.

Such vessels were marked with red crosses to distinguish them from combat ships. In the case of the Australian hospital ship AHS *Centaur,* a Japanese submarine ignored its markings. The sub torpedoed and sank the ship in May 1943. A German hospital ship, the former ocean liner *Deutschland,* was not properly marked when British planes mistakenly attacked it in 1945. The *Deutschland* sunk.

Though clearly marked has a hospital ship, the AHS *Centaur* was sunk by a Japanese submarine on May 14, 1943, off the coast of Queensland, Australia, just east of Brisbane.

Above, a group of nurses sprint down a beach in gas masks as part of their training. Nurses, doctors, and other medical personnel had to be ready for just about every battlefield situation.

Sometimes vessels, such as the liner shown at right, were transformed into floating hospitals. These ships could care for large numbers of wounded soldiers while simultaneously taking them to safer facilities away from the fighting.

War in the Air

World War I was a period of testing and early development of air power, but World War II saw air power transform into an essential and devastating military weapon. At sea, especially in the Pacific, warplanes could destroy even the largest battleships. On land, the military with the strongest air support had a key advantage.

Yet, it was civilians who seemed to suffer most from air attack. In Germany as well as in Britain, cities were bombed to ruins, and under those ruins were thousands of civilian casualties. Allied and Axis bombers struck populated areas, intending to inflict civilian losses. This strategy was meant to terrorize the enemy's population and break its will to fight.

Yet, this "strategic bombing" of cities did not succeed until the very end of the war, when atomic bombs finally forced Japan's unconditional surrender.

Throughout the European theater of war, Axis and Allied airfields sent their bombers to attack enemy bases and industrial centers. Bombers carried as many as eight machine guns for protection and were escorted by fighter planes that battled enemy fighters. Bombers were in danger of being shot down by anti-aircraft guns that filled the skies with exploding shells.

A group of TBF Avenger bombers fly in formation during a training exercise in 1942. Avengers saw a lot of action in World War II, most notably during the Battle of Midway in the Pacific.

THE UNBORN NAZI JET

THE MAIN DISADVANTAGE German fighter pilots faced was the need to fly long distances to attack Allied bases such as those in Great Britain.

After flying long distances, German fighters were short of fuel when they went into action with enemy planes. Allied fighters conserved fuel by waiting until the last minute to take off before challenging Nazi warplanes.

Throughout the war, German inventors worked on a jet engine that would have given their warplanes an unmatched advantage over Allied planes. Tests on the Messerschmitt Me-262 were being conducted by summer 1942. Jet engines did not, however, go into production in time to help Germany in the air war.

Though it was being developed at the outset of World War II, the Me-262 jet arrived too late to help the Germans.

BOMBING RAIDS

THE GERMAN *LUFTWAFFE'S* defeat in the 1940 Battle of Britain was in part because their Messerschmitt fighter escorts did not have the flying range to stay with their bombers. German bombing of England continued, but by 1943 the Allies were causing more damage than they suffered.

Still, RAF losses were so heavy that only nighttime raids were carried out until the US Army Air Force arrived in mid-1942. At first, the Americans chose to fly during the day, when it was easier to see their targets. The result, however, was high US losses in crews and aircraft.

The Hawker Hurricane fighter was invaluable to the RAF throughout the Battle of Britain. Though it was slower than its German counterpart, the Messerschmitt, it held its own. It scored more than half of the RAF's victories as England withstood the German assault and won the battle.

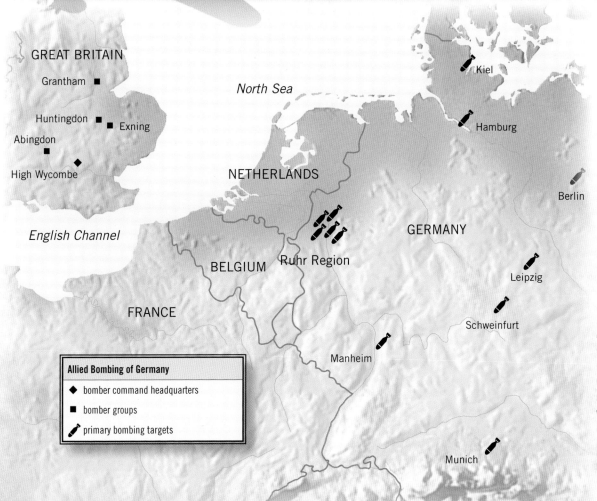

GREAT BRITAIN

Grantham ■

North Sea

Huntingdon ■ ■ Exning

Abingdon ■

High Wycombe ◆

Kiel

Hamburg

Berlin

NETHERLANDS

English Channel

Ruhr Region

GERMANY

BELGIUM

Leipzig

FRANCE

Schweinfurt

Manheim

Allied Bombing of Germany

◆ bomber command headquarters

■ bomber groups

⬗ primary bombing targets

Munich

Allied bombing raids on Germany focused heavily on industrial regions where weapons and munitions factories were located. Most of these missions originated at RAF bases in England.

Fortress Europe

Nazi Germany constructed strong defenses along occupied Europe's western coastline, called *Festung Europa,* or "Fortress Europe," in German. Known as the Atlantic Wall, these works ran from France's border with Spain to the northern reaches of Norway.

The Atlantic Wall employed concrete fortifications, underwater obstacles, barbed wire, minefields, and bunkers for antitank guns, machine guns, and artillery. The French coast alone had more than six million mines. Gun fortifications were dug into cliff faces, while huge blockhouses had guns that could be withdrawn, disappearing from sight. The purpose was to stop or slow any Allied invasion long enough for Axis forces to counterattack.

While Allied troops were struggling out of their landing craft, trying to break through the

Strong German defenses along the Atlantic coastline presented a tremendous challenge to the Allies. Reinforced gun positions, such as this one in Longues-sur-Mer, France, withstood heavy Allied bombing and remain in place today.

WAR DATA

IN AUGUST 1942, the Allies resolved to test the Atlantic Wall by mounting a major raid on the French resort town of Dieppe. The mission of the 6,100-strong attack force, mainly Canadian troops, was to seize the seaport while also testing new weapons and amphibious landing methods.

Poor planning made the task impossible. Despite air and sea bombardments, Nazi defenses remained effective, and the *Luftwaffe* outfought the Allied warplanes. Many troops never got off the beaches but were slaughtered by gunfire from the fortifications.

Of the 5,000 men who reached shore, only 1,650 returned to the invasion fleet.

fortifications, they would come under heavy artillery barrage and machine-gun fire. If not wiped out on the beach, the attackers would be pushed back into the sea.

When General Eisenhower took command of Allied forces in Europe in 1942, he and his staff began studying the Atlantic Wall for an eventual invasion of Europe. These defenses were strongest on the French Pas-de-Calais coast, which was closest to England. After deciding where to invade, the Allies had to develop the equipment required to successfully do it.

Concentration Camp Locations

■ concentration camp

North
Sea

DENMARK

Baltic
Sea

UNITED
KINGDOM

Bergen-Belsen   Ravensbruck   Stutthoff   Treblinka

NETHER-
LANDS

Mittelbau   Chelmo   Sobibor

Vught   Sachsenhausen   Maidanek

Buchenwald

Gross-Rosen   POLAND

GERMANY   Belzec

Theresienstadt   Auschwitz-
Birkenau

Flossenburg   CZECHOSLOVAKIA

Natzweiler   Dachau   Mauthausen

FRANCE   SWITZ.   AUSTRIA   HUNGARY

BELGIUM

DID YOU KNOW?

While millions of Jews were imprisoned and killed in other Axis countries, Japan was a safe haven for Jewish refugees. In the 1930s, Japan first welcomed Jews fleeing anti-Semitic persecution in Europe, especially from Germany. Considering them valuable additions to Imperial Japanese society, the government refused Nazi demands to persecute these new immigrants.

THE HOLOCAUST

OCCUPIED EUROPE was not just a fortress in 1943: it was also the scene of ruthless Nazi oppression and murder. The victims were Jews, communists, homosexuals, and Gypsies.

Europe's Jews suffered most, with almost 5.8 million executed or dying of disease or starvation in concentration camps. By June 1942, the world was hearing about poison gas being used on Jewish prisoners in "death camps." Three million Polish and one million Soviet Jews died. The number of Jewish deaths elsewhere was also appalling. In Romania, 469,000 died; in Czechoslovakia, 277,000; in the Baltic States, 222,000; in Hungary, 200,000; in Germany, 160,000, and in the Netherlands, 106,000.

Jews call this period the Holocaust, or "firestorm."

The concentration camp in Auschwitz, Poland, was the largest of all such camps and was responsible for the deaths of more than one million people. Above the front gates of the notorious facility are the words *"Arbeit Macht Frei,"* which loosely translated means, "Work shall set you free." Today, the camp is a museum and constant reminder of the atrocities committed during World War II.

Kursk: The Last Eastern Offensive

Soviet operations in the winter of 1942–43 slowed down after the victory at Stalingrad in February. Then, the Germans launched a major counterattack that retook the city of Kharkov.

The Nazi forces had been severely weakened, while the Soviets were being supplied and equipped by their allies. American merchant ships journeyed northward through icy seas to the port of Murmansk, where tanks, guns, and equipment were landed. While new Soviet recruits replaced the millions of casualties, the Axis forces on the Eastern Front did not have enough troops to replace their losses.

Still, Hitler ordered his armies to prepare a massive new offensive against the Soviets in late spring 1943. His forces moved against Kursk, but Stalin anticipated this move. The Soviets were fortified, and their armor was ready to meet the Nazi advance head-on.

Meanwhile, behind German lines that April, Jewish civilians in Warsaw rose up against the Nazis. Deportation had reduced the city's original Jewish population of 450,000 to 60,000. The remaining people lived in the Jewish quarter, known as the Warsaw Ghetto.

The Nazis crushed their desperate uprising, killing 13,000 Jewish residents. Most survivors were deported to concentration camps.

DID YOU KNOW?

Hitler's enormous armies on the Eastern Front included hundreds of thousands of troops from the smaller Axis countries. Nearly 800,000 Romanians, for example, fought for Germany in the Soviet campaigns. More than 300,000 Romanian military personnel died in the war, most fighting the Soviets.

In the Battle of Kursk, German forces once again used a blitzkrieg attack in hopes of catching Russian troops off guard and surrounding them. But, after withstanding the initial German assault, the Soviets countered with a well-planned offensive of their own that lasted almost a month.

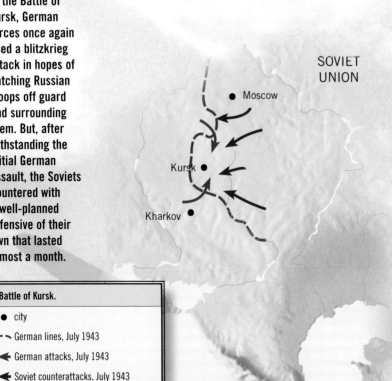

SOVIET UNION

Moscow

Kursk

Kharkov

Battle of Kursk.

● city

- German lines, July 1943

← German attacks, July 1943

← Soviet counterattacks, July 1943

THE GREATEST TANK BATTLE

IN JULY 1943, Hitler's commanders at Kursk counted on blitzkrieg tactics to shatter the Soviet forces. Two massive pincer movements were to close behind the defenders and surround them. Instead of the pincers meeting, however, they were blocked by minefields. Then came the armored counterattack led by Marshal Zhukov, the Soviet hero of Leningrad and Stalingrad.

More than 900,000 Axis troops with 3,000 tanks faced 1.3 million Soviets with 3,600 tanks. After ten days that included the greatest tank battle of the war, the Nazis had lost more than half their armor. Hitler, himself, ordered an end to the offensive. The blitzkrieg was defeated.

In one of the most memorable images from World War II, German soldiers pull residents of the Warsaw Ghetto into the street as German troops move to crush the revolt that saw Jews resist deportation to death camps. Though the uprising lasted several months, in the end, the rebels had too few guns and not enough supplies to fight off the German soldiers.

Il Duce Gets the Boot

In North Africa, Rommel's German and Italian troops fought hard for Tunisia before surrendering in May 1943. More than 250,000 Axis forces were captured. Rommel escaped to lead the defense of Fortress Europe. Eisenhower now turned to the buildup for an invasion of Mussolini's Italy. The invasion began in July with an amphibious attack on the island of Sicily, at the toe of the Italian peninsula's "boot." By now, the Italian people were sick of the war, as bombs fell on their cities, including the capital, Rome. The Italian army was close to collapse, and Mussolini soon lost the support of Italy's ruling Fascist Party. The tyrant once known as *Il Duce* was ousted from office and

THE ANZIO INVASION

GERMAN-LED RESISTANCE to the Allied invasion of Italy was both fierce and skillful. The mountains and rivers of Italy made the advance slow and bloody. Strongholds such as the monastery at Monte Cassino stopped attack after attack.

In January 1944, the Allies landed a force at Anzio, just south of Rome. The plan was to get behind German defenders, forcing them to retreat. The Allies met strong resistance at Anzio, however, and were pinned down on a small beachhead for three months.

The Allies finally broke out of Anzio in May, Monte Cassino also fell, and the Germans withdrew northward.

arrested on the orders of King Victor Emmanuel III. The Italian government began secret peace negotiations with the Allies—even though thousands of Nazi troops occupied their country.

By mid-August, Sicily fell to Montgomery's British Eighth Army and the US Seventh Army, commanded by General George S. Patton, Jr. (1889–1945). The invasion of mainland Italy began on September 3. Soon afterward, German paratroopers rescued Mussolini from prison. Reinstated as leader of a new government, he was just a puppet to Adolf Hitler.

Nicknamed "Old Blood and Guts," General George S. Patton was a gruff veteran of World War I and an expert in tank warfare. After making a name for himself in North Africa, Patton was given command of the US Seventh Army for the invasion of Sicily.

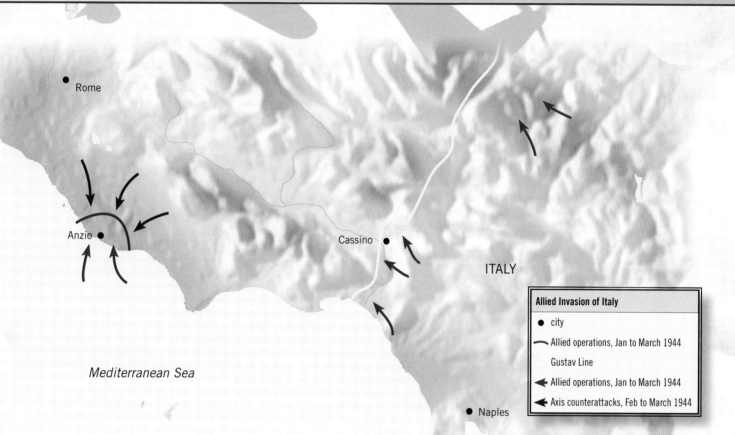

Rome

Anzio

Cassino

ITALY

Mediterranean Sea

Naples

Allied Invasion of Italy

● city

⌐ Allied operations, Jan to March 1944

Gustav Line

◄ Allied operations, Jan to March 1944

◄ Axis counterattacks, Feb to March 1944

Though Allied troops had little trouble capturing the island of Sicily, they met with much stiffer resistance from German forces on the Italian mainland. The Allies were pinned down at Anzio for months and also had trouble breaking through the German defensive front known as the Gustav Line as they advanced toward the town of Cassino.

MUSSOLINI'S FATE

BY LATE 1944, Benito Mussolini had few friends on his side. The Germans were disgusted that he could not keep the Italian government in the war, and Italian anti-fascist fighting forces wanted to see him dead.

Officially, Mussolini was head of a pro-Nazi Italian government, but most of his country had made a truce with the Allies and declared war on the Nazis. In April 1945, with his cause clearly lost, Mussolini and his mistress tried to escape by airplane to Spain. Instead, Italian communist partisans (guerrillas) caught and executed them.

On the heels of the initial invasion of Italy, the Allied landings at Anzio in January 1944 were code-named Operation Shingle. The amphibious landings themselves went mostly unopposed, but German troops quickly gathered themselves and were able to hem Allied forces in on the beach. It would take four months for Allies to break out of Anzio.

Storming the Beaches

The Allied invasion of Fortress Europe, Operation Overlord, hit France's northern coast in Normandy on June 6, 1944. Known as D-Day, it started with 23,000 paratroopers landing at night by parachute and gliders behind German lines.

Almost 2,500 ships transported an invasion force of 108,000 American, British, and Canadian soldiers. Warplanes flew 14,000 attacks on the first day alone. Eisenhower was Supreme Allied Commander, and the ground troops were led by Britain's Bernard Montgomery.

The few thousand German defenders fought stubbornly, firing artillery and machine guns at the thousands of troop-filled landing craft plowing through the surf toward four beaches. The Allies quickly pushed past beaches code-named Gold, Juno, and Sword, but at Omaha their losses were especially heavy.

DID YOU KNOW?

The name Jeep was first used for the four-wheel-drive "General Purpose" or "G.P.," vehicle developed for the US Army around 1940. More than 640,000 Jeeps were manufactured during the war.

Wave after wave of Allied soldiers landed at Normandy, with many in the first groups ultimately sacrificing their lives for those yet to come.

THE BREAKOUT

POWERFUL GERMAN FORCES assembled to keep the Allied invasion force trapped on the Normandy peninsula. The fighting was savage among the hedgerows and fields of Normandy, where German machine guns and dug-in tanks fought for every foot.

The US Third Army, under General Patton, led the breakout in late July. Patton's force of tanks and troop carriers advanced after heavy Allied air bombardments of the St. Lo region of Normandy. Allied forces broke out at St. Lo and surrounded pockets of German troops or forced them back.

In mid-August, a second invasion of France took place, this time on its southern coast on the Mediterranean.

The invasion took place along 60 miles of rugged coastline. The Allies fought their way inland before large enemy reinforcements could arrive. D-Day succeeded in part because the German high command believed the real attack would be farther north, and strong forces were positioned there, instead. Nazi generals Karl von Rundstedt (1875–1953) and Rommel at first delayed in counterattacking because they thought Normandy was not the main invasion.

By late July, in less than eight weeks since D-Day, the Allies had landed almost 1.5 million troops and began to break out of the Normandy peninsula.

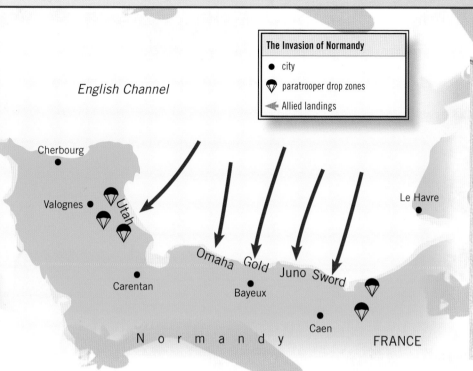

The Invasion of Normandy

● city

◈ paratrooper drop zones

◄ Allied landings

English Channel

Cherbourg

Valognes

Utah

Omaha Gold Juno Sword

Carentan

Bayeux

Caen

Le Havre

N o r m a n d y   FRANCE

SLAUGHTER ON OMAHA BEACH

ON D-DAY, the US Army's 1st and 29th infantry divisions and Army Rangers waded ashore through the Omaha Beach surf. Their landing craft grounded or were blocked by underwater obstacles such as steel gates and mines. Heavy enemy fire from bluffs above immediately cut down hundreds of Americans.

Artillery shells exploded among the invaders, who were pinned down as soon as they reached shore. Rangers scaled the bluffs and cleared out enemy positions, and Allied naval guns blasted the defenders. The infantry kept moving forward, but as night fell, they had advanced only one mile. That mile cost 8,600 killed and wounded Americans.

As part of the invasion of Normandy, Allied forces crossed the English Channel and landed on beaches code-named Sword, Juno, Gold, Omaha, and Utah. Along with these amphibious assaults there were also Allied airborne landings behind the eastern and western ends of the beaches.

In the photo below, American troops exit their landing craft and wade in toward Omaha Beach in chest-deep waters as part of the Normandy landings. Contending with heavy shelling from German defenses and not many places to find cover, this invasion was every bit as scary as it looks.

Closing In on Japan

The Allies referred to the conflict with Japan as the Pacific War. For Japan, it was part of the Greater East Asia War, its struggle with China and war with the Western powers.

While Allied and Japanese infantry and marines slugged it out island-to-island, their air forces and navies battled to control the skies and the seas. The troops had to be transported and supplied by sea, but aircraft were needed to destroy enemy shipping or protect their own. And below the surface, submarines attacked supply vessels and troop transports as well as warships.

As the Allies captured islands ever closer to Japan, airfields were built on those islands from which bombers could reach Japanese cities. Aircraft from those fields could combine with carrier planes and attack Japanese fleets with overwhelming power. In mid-June 1944, American pilots won the Battle of the Philippine Sea. They shot down more than 500 Japanese planes and sank three carriers.

With the capture of the Mariana Islands that summer, American B-29 bombers now had airfields within easy reach of Japan. These fields were also used to support the invasion of the Philippines in October. But, first came the massive Battle of Leyte Gulf.

This map shows the areas where the four major engagements in the Battle of Leyte Gulf took place. Altogether, the fighting in Leyte Gulf proved to be the largest naval battle in history.

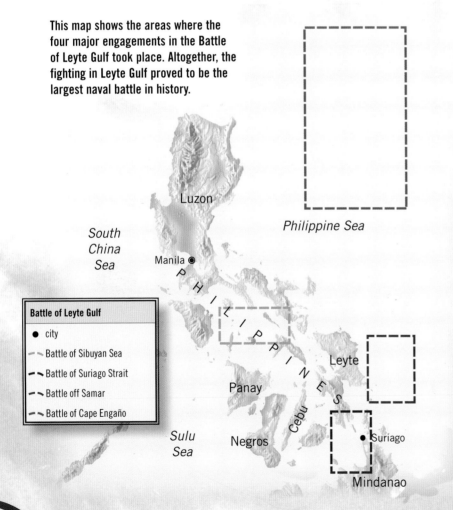

Battle of Leyte Gulf
- ● city
- ⌁ Battle of Sibuyan Sea
- ⌁ Battle of Suriago Strait
- ⌁ Battle off Samar
- ⌁ Battle of Cape Engaño

LEYTE GULF

IN OCTOBER 1944, Admiral Nimitz and General MacArthur headed for the Philippines with 750 ships and 160,000 troops.

Few Japanese carriers remained after the Philippine Sea defeat, but four were placed to attract a US attack. If the Americans took the bait, another Japanese fleet under Admiral Takeo Kurita (1889–1977) would sink the unprotected US troop transports.

The US Third Fleet of Admiral William F. Halsey (1882–1959) sank the carriers. Meanwhile, the US Australian Seventh Fleet under Admiral Thomas C. Kinkaid (1888–1972) stopped the main attack by Kurita's fleet. The Battle of Leyte Gulf, history's largest naval battle, also cost Japan three battleships and 500 planes.

The Battle of Saipan in the Marianas was fought in June and July 1944. On the oppsite page right, a photo shows, a US Marine coming upon a woman and her children, Saipan natives, who had taken shelter during the fighting.

DID YOU KNOW?

The Battle of Leyte Gulf saw the first Japanese suicide air attacks, called *kamikaze,* or "divine wind." Pilots flew their explosives-filled warplanes into ships in hopes of sinking them. More than 3,900 kamikaze pilots sacrificed themselves in this way during the war.

WAR DATA

AS AN ISLAND NATION, Japan depended on ships for raw materials, food, and especially oil. In 1944, Allied submarines in the Pacific—mainly the US Navy's 150 subs—sank 650 Japanese vessels. At least 124 were oil tankers, causing Japan's military and industry to run short of fuel.

By the end of the war, Allied submarines had sunk 1,200 Japanese merchant ships. Submarines sank more than 200 Japanese warships, including eight aircraft carriers and a battleship. More than 150 Japanese submarines were lost, while the US Navy lost forty-two submarines.

The Irresistible Soviet War Machine

 As other Allied forces crushed the Axis in Italy, France, and the Pacific in 1944, huge Soviet offensives attacked the Axis from the East. The siege of Leningrad was lifted after two and a half years, but a million Soviets had died there from starvation and wounds.

The Soviets had little sympathy for the thousands of Axis troops they took prisoner. On their eastward invasions, the Axis had executed or starved to death millions of prisoners. By the time their counteroffensive was over, the Soviets would be responsible for the deaths of 600,000 captives.

The battlefield valor of Axis and Soviet fighters made the Eastern European campaigns of 1944 extremely brutal and bloody. Hitler called on his troops to fight to the death. Stalin demanded the capture of Berlin itself and the utter defeat of Hitler.

In mid-1944 more than 1.2 million Soviet troops struck the Axis center. Soviet war hero Marshal Konstantin Rokossovsky (1896–1968) planned this offensive and commanded frontline troops. In six weeks, Hitler's forces retreated 300 miles. By September, the Soviet Union was liberated, and the front line was in Poland, Hungary, and Romania. Polish resistance forces rose up against the Germans in Warsaw, but they were betrayed by the Soviets, who did not come to their aid.

DID YOU KNOW?

Finland was a "co-belligerent" Axis ally but not a formal signer of the Axis pact, or agreement. Finland battled Soviet invasions until the two countries agreed to a truce in September 1944.

BETRAYAL OF WARSAW

AS SOVIET GUNS bombarded German positions near Warsaw in August 1944, Polish resistance forces prepared an uprising. Fearing the Nazis would destroy Warsaw as they left, the Polish Underground Army decided to drive the enemy out. Already, Soviet tanks were breaking into the city and warplanes were bombing Nazi positions.

The Poles attacked the German troops and radioed the Soviets to support them immediately. The Germans sent five divisions into Warsaw, but Stalin did not advance. Instead, he allowed these Polish patriots to be wiped out. In this way, resistance forces would be eliminated when he took control of Poland.

A member of the Polish resistance movement defends his position during the Warsaw uprising. Though Soviet troops could have helped struggling resistance fighters, Joseph Stalin held his forces back and left the Poles at the mercy of the Germans.

Operation Bagration

- • city
- ◄ Soviet offenses, June to Dec 1944
- — German lines, June 1944
- ⌒ German lines, Dec 1944

Moscow

SOVIET
UNION

Berlin

GERMANY

Kiev

Carpathian Mountains

ROMANIA

THE SOVIET BATTLE TANK

HUNDREDS OF American-made Sherman tanks helped the Soviets fight the Nazis, but a Soviet-built tank, the T-34, was Stalin's main armored weapon. War factories behind Soviet lines turned out tens of thousands of formidable T-34s.

Like the famed German Tiger Tank, the T-34 was equipped with an accurate cannon that made it deadly at long distances. The T-34 was also fast and mobile, designed for blitzkrieg tactics. Considered by many to be World War II's finest tank, it was the most-produced tank of the war. For years to come, the T-34 influenced armor design and production in many countries.

The Soviet-made T-34 tank like the one shown below, was widely regarded as one of the best tanks in World War II. Its combination of speed, mobility, and accuracy influenced tank designs for years to come.

Operation Bagration was the name given to the Soviet offensive that smashed the German Army Group Center. More than one million Russian soldiers, assembled from the Baltic Sea to the Carpathian Mountain range, pushed the German lines back hundreds of miles in just a few short months. The German army would never fully recover from its losses here.

Germany's Desperate Counterattack

 Through 1944, Allied forces pushed the Germans slowly back across Western Europe. Short of troops, Hitler drafted boys in their early teens to serve in home defense services such as antiaircraft units. Still, the German military fought hard—though it was caught in a vice between the Soviets and the Western Allies.

Paris fell at the end of August, and Free French forces led by General Charles de Gaulle (1890–1970) had the honor of liberating the joyous city. Also involved in the liberation of Paris was highly admired American General Omar N. Bradley (1893–1981), who commanded an army group of 1.3 million troops.

In the Battle of the Bulge, Hitler's troops surprised the Allies in the Ardennes forest with an offensive launched on December 16, 1944. Though the Germans made significant progress, by early January, their offensive stalled, and soon thereafter, Allied counterattacks ended the threat.

Above, paratroopers fill the sky as part of Operation Market Garden, which was a failed Allied attempt to take back strategic locations in the German-occupied Netherlands.

All did not go well for the Allies, however. That September, a massive parachute drop, Operation Market Garden, behind enemy lines near Arnhem in the Netherlands was cut off and destroyed. Of more than 10,000 paratroopers, only 2,800 returned to Allied lines.

As the Allies prepared to break through into Germany that winter, Hitler readied a surprise. More than 250,000 troops and all the armor the Germans could assemble stormed American troops in the Ardennes forest. The Battle of the Bulge—named for the depth of the German breakthrough—ended in January with the defeat of Hitler's attacking force.

Soldiers of the United States 28th Infantry Division, shown on opposite page, take a triumphant march down the famed Champs-Elysées in Paris, France.

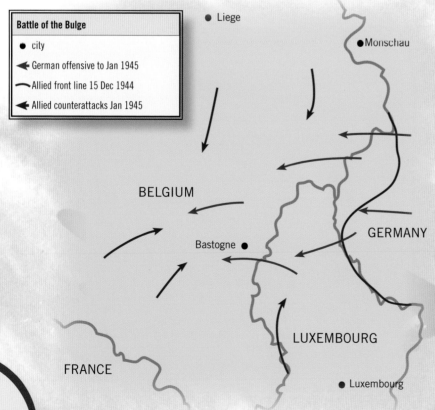

Battle of the Bulge

- ● city
- ◄— German offensive to Jan 1945
- —— Allied front line 15 Dec 1944
- ◄— Allied counterattacks Jan 1945

● Liege

●Monschau

BELGIUM

Bastogne ●

GERMANY

LUXEMBOURG

FRANCE

● Luxembourg

THE MANHATTAN PROJECT

SINCE EARLY IN THE WAR, both Allied and German scientists worked to build a nuclear bomb. German-born American physicist Albert Einstein (1879–1955) had inspired the Allied research. Einstein theorized that the element uranium could be used to make history's most powerful explosive device.

Creating an atomic bomb was the task of the top-secret Manhattan Project. By mid-1945, a bomb had been tested in the New Mexico desert. Axis bomb development did not succeed, but the Allies were now ready to use their devastating new weapon. The question was whether to use it against Germany or Japan or both.

WAR DATA

ONE OF THE LAST Nazi hopes in 1944–45 was a robotic "flying bomb," a rocket that could reach British cities. Intended to demoralize enemy civilians, these were termed V-weapons, for *Vergeltungswaffen*, or "revenge weapons."

V-1 rockets could fly up to 400 miles per hour and carried an 1,800-pound explosive. The later V-2 rockets traveled at 4,000 miles per hour, with a 2,000-pound bomb. V-1 rockets could be shot down by fighter planes or antiaircraft guns, but there was no defense against the V-2s. Allied bombings and captures of their launching sites finally put an end to these ultramodern revenge weapons.

As Germany struggled to hold off the Allies, they turned their attention to creating V-weapons, such as the rocket shown at right. They had long-range capabilities and proved to be the blueprint for missiles now used in modern warfare.

Victory in Europe

As the Allies battled across Germany in 1945, President Roosevelt died unexpectedly on April 12. Serving his fourth term as president, Roosevelt had been in declining health. He died of a brain hemorrhage. The loss of such a strong and capable leader shocked Roosevelt's many admirers in the free world. Vice President Harry S. Truman (1884–1972) succeeded him.

On April 25, American troops reached the Elbe River, joining with Soviet soldiers. Fighting continued, as Western and Soviet troops advanced in Czechoslovakia and Austria. German forces in northern Italy surrendered on April 29.

DID YOU KNOW?

Famous American big band leader Glenn Miller went missing in December 1944 while entertaining troops in France. Miller's airplane disappeared in bad weather and was never found.

The Soviets stormed through Berlin, fighting hand-to-hand, street-to-street. Isolated in a bunker in the center of the city, Hitler committed suicide on April 30.

Utterly defeated, the remaining German generals surrendered to the Western Allies on May 7, and to the Soviets on May 8. The combined Allied forces, formally fighting as the United Nations, had at last defeated Nazi Germany— until then the possessors of the world's most powerful military.

The meaning of military power soon would change, however, as the Allies turned their attentions to Japan. Soon the mushroom-shaped clouds of nuclear bombs would announce the dawn of the Atomic Age.

Two US soldiers hustle across a square in Kronach, Germany, as a gasoline trailer behind them shoots flames skyward.

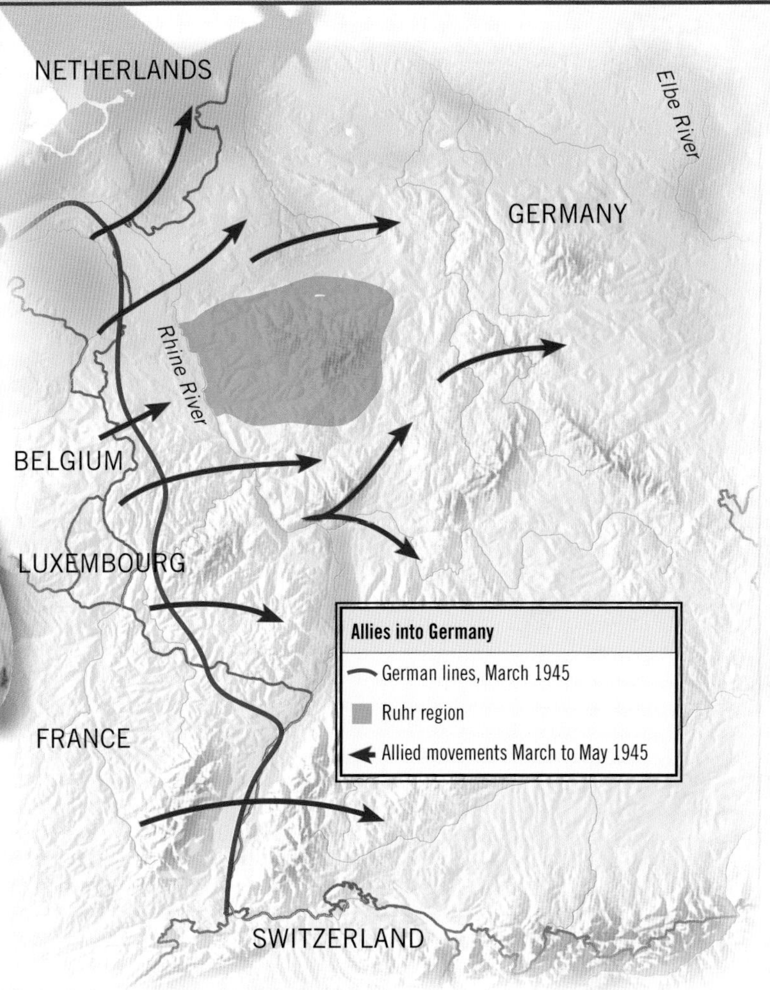

NETHERLANDS

GERMANY

Elbe River

Rhine River

BELGIUM

LUXEMBOURG

Allies into Germany
— German lines, March 1945
■ Ruhr region
◄— Allied movements March to May 1945

FRANCE

SWITZERLAND

Above, Second Lieutenant William Robertson of the US Army shares a smile and embrace with his Russian ally, Lieutenant Alexander Sylvashko, as the two armies meet up in Germany.

Though the Germans managed to destroy many of the bridges spanning the Rhine River (map at right) into Germany, the Allies were still able to break through their defenses. In late March 1945, over 300,000 German soldiers surrendered in the Ruhr region of the country.

NUREMBERG TRIALS

BY NOVEMBER 1945, the International Military Tribunal, composed of British, French, American, and Soviet judges had brought to trial and convicted twenty-four top Nazi leaders with war crimes. The tribunal was held in the German city Nuremberg.

The defendants were accused of crimes against peace (starting a war of aggression), crimes against humanity (exterminations and deportations), and violations of the laws of war. Among accused was former Luftwaffe commander, Herman Göring, who committed suicide by poison while in his cell.

Three defendants were acquitted, twelve were sentenced to death, and others were sentenced to prolonged imprisonment.

Among the Nazi leaders who were brought to trial to answer for their war crimes was Herman Göring (front row, far left), who was the head of the Luftwaffe and second in command to Hitler.

Imperial Japan Fights On

Although suffering enormous losses, and with her cities bombed to ruins, Japan refused to surrender. Even the defeat of Germany did not convince the Japanese to ask for peace terms. And as far as the Allies were concerned, there would be no terms other than unconditional surrender.

The Allies were eliminating Japanese forces in campaigns from the Philippines to Indochina. Between February and June, US troops assaulted the island strongholds of Iwo Jima and Okinawa. More than 130,000 Japanese and almost 20,000 Americans died in this fighting, some of the most savage of the war.

By June 1945, Japan had enemies on every side. Chinese forces on mainland Asia had turned back Japanese offensives and were on the attack. US submarines were in the Sea of Japan, where they sank twenty-eight vessels.

A Corsair fighter plane fires its rockets at Japanese positions during the Battle of Okinawa.

Allied strategic bombing campaigns were dropping explosives that unleashed firestorms and destroyed fifty-eight urban areas. Almost 700,000 citizens were casualties, with nine million left homeless.

Japan began to communicate secretly with the Soviets, with whom they were still at peace. The Japanese wanted to make terms with the Allies. It was estimated that an invasion of Japan would cost the lives of many hundreds of thousands on both sides.

After being forced out of the Philippines in 1942, General Douglas MacArthur uttered the famous line, "I shall return." As this photo testifies, he made good on his promise. Along with other officers, MacArthur waded ashore at Leyte Island in October 1944.

IWO JIMA AND OKINAWA

IN THE PHILIPPINES, Japanese troops would fight on until the end of the war. Meanwhile, in February 1945, American forces moved against the islands of Iwo Jima and Okinawa. Airfields here would be within 350 to 600 miles of Japan.

Iwo Jima, 8 square miles defended by 25,000 troops, was assaulted first. US marines fought for the island from mid-February through late March, at a cost of 25,000 US casualties. Virtually all of the Japanese combatants on Okinawa, with its 100,000 defenders, died.

From April 1 to June 30, 290,000 Allied troops supported by 1,500 vessels assaulted Okinawa. There were 50,000 Allied casualties, while no Japanese survived.

Iwo Jima, with its two airfields and close proximity to Japan's mainland, was of great strategic importance to the Allies. The first wave of marines landed in February 1945, and, on March 26, the last of the Japanese troops went down fighting on the northern tip of the island.

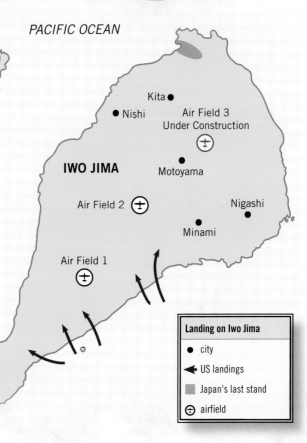

PACIFIC OCEAN

Kita
Nishi
Air Field 3
Under Construction

IWO JIMA

Motoyama

Air Field 2

Nigashi

Minami

Air Field 1

Landing on Iwo Jima
- city
- US landings
- Japan's last stand
- airfield

In one of the most famous images from World War II, US Marines raise the American flag on the island of Iwo Jima. Though the flag-raising provided a proud moment, the battle was hardly over. In fact, three of the six men who raised the flag ended up dying on Iwo Jima.

Victory in the Pacific

With the defeat of Germany and Italy, Allied troops and war supplies were transported from Europe to the Pacific. In July, Allied leaders met in Potsdam, Germany, to decide their next step.

Urgent Japanese messages requested that the Soviets help broker a peace deal, but the Allies demanded complete and immediate surrender. To avoid the bloodshed an invasion would bring, the United States resolved to drop nuclear weapons on Japan.

No one really knew what would happen when an atomic device was exploded. Would it even destroy the aircraft, itself? Dangerous radiation from the blasts was still little-understood. Even a number of scientists who helped develop it were opposed. Still, plans went ahead.

On August 6, a B-29 Superfortress with a nuclear bomb left its base in the Mariana Islands. The target city was Hiroshima, on southern Japan. The bomb was equal to 20,000 tons of high explosives. More than 70,000 people were killed, with another 125,000 eventually dying from wounds or radiation.

The Japanese did not immediately surrender. On August 8, the Soviets declared war on Japan and invaded Manchuria. One day later, August 9, the United States dropped a second nuclear bomb. The city of Nagasaki suffered similar deadly results. Within days, Emperor Hirohito asked for peace.

World War II was over.

SURRENDER ON THE *MISSOURI*

THE JAPANESE surrender officially took place in Tokyo Bay on September 2, 1945, aboard the newest American battleship, USS *Missouri*.

Representatives of the Japanese government and military attended the ceremony, which opened with General MacArthur's address—a hope for future "freedom, tolerance, and justice." Japan was soon disarmed and the country occupied by Allied forces under MacArthur's command.

In Japan and most countries, the official end of World War II was August 15, when Emperor Hirohito's surrender statement was broadcast over the radio.

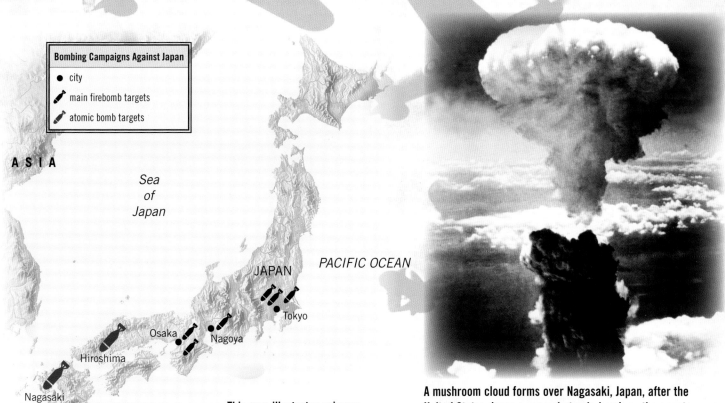

Bombing Campaigns Against Japan
- ● city
- ✈ main firebomb targets
- ✈ atomic bomb targets

ASIA

Sea of Japan

JAPAN

PACIFIC OCEAN

Tokyo

Osaka

Nagoya

Hiroshima

Nagasaki

This map illustrates primary Allied bombing targets in Japan.

A mushroom cloud forms over Nagasaki, Japan, after the United States drops a second atomic bomb on the country. Soon thereafter, Japan surrendered.

THE POTSDAM CONFERENCE

THE FUTURE of the world hung in the balance as Allied leaders met in Potsdam, July 17–August 2, 1945. Plans were laid to divide conquered Europe between the Western Allies and the Soviets. Although the Western countries wanted freedom for the lands they occupied, the Soviets intended to turn Eastern Europe into communist dictatorships under Stalin's rule.

With Stalin at Potsdam were President Truman and Prime Minister Churchill. During the conference, a British election removed Churchill's party from power. He was replaced by new Prime Minister, Clement Attlee (1883–1967).

Plans also were made at Potsdam to force Japan's surrender.

New British prime minister Clement Attlee (left) takes a seat alongside Harry Truman and Joseph Stalin at the Potsdam Conference. At the meeting, plans were made as to the fate of defeated Axis countries and what to do about Japan.

New Roles in Society

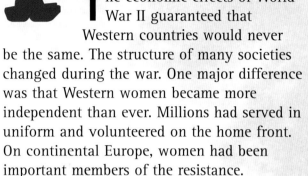 The economic effects of World War II guaranteed that Western countries would never be the same. The structure of many societies changed during the war. One major difference was that Western women became more independent than ever. Millions had served in uniform and volunteered on the home front. On continental Europe, women had been important members of the resistance.

Pictured above, women in Florida trade in their housework and office jobs for a pair of goggles as they take a training course in war-related work. The outbreak of World War II went a long way in changing the way women were perceived in many societies.

Once war broke out, it didn't take long for women to step in and take on jobs that men had previously held. At left, three American women working in a shipyard toil diligently on one of the vessels.

In Britain, the Women's Land Army was organized to put tens of thousands of young women to work in agriculture. American women worked on industrial production lines, making munitions and working on warplanes and ships. Jobs that once were considered for men only now had to be done by women—and they were done with skill and efficiency. Other women headed their families when men were away, often planting vegetable gardens to provide enough food and raising children alone.

By the end of the war, American and British women in particular had achieved a certain financial independence that no other

Perhaps the most recognizable example of the brave service of black soldiers during the war were the men of the 332nd Fighter Group, known as the Tuskegee Airmen.

A NEW HORIZON IN AMERICA

AMERICAN INDUSTRIAL GROWTH and prosperity sprang out of the effort to supply and equip the greatest militaries ever seen.

One major social change was the expanding role of African Americans in the military and workforce. All-black units served gallantly in battle, including ace fighter pilot squadrons. At home, many black workers were protected by new government policies that forbade racial discrimination in defense industries.

Although these jobs ended as wartime industry shut down, African Americans who had fought and worked for victory now demanded full civil rights and a fair share of their country's prosperity.

African American women back home often worked for war-related concerns, such as this riveter with Lockheed Aircraft.

LABOR IN WARTIME

ONE OF GERMANY'S economic disadvantages was its policy banning women from the industrial workforce. In the United States, Britain, and the Soviet Union, millions of women took essential war-production jobs while men were in the service.

Germany, instead, used the forced labor of prisoners of war and captives taken from concentration camps. The Japanese also had labor camps, using military and civilian prisoners, many of whom died.

The voluntary labor of women working for their home countries was far more effective than forced labor.

generation had known. With the return of men to the peacetime workforce, most women had to give up their jobs at first. Within a few years, they were employed once more, as economies boomed and they were needed in the workforce.

The UN and Cold War

From the ashes of World War II arose a new international organization dedicated to peace, justice, and prosperity. The United Nations replaced the former League of Nations in October 1945. The original twenty-six nations who established the UN in 1942 were now joined by new members for a total of fifty-one countries.

The tasks of reconstruction and peacemaking were immense. They required US financing and the cooperation of the UN member states. The world soon was again divided into two hostile camps: the Communist Bloc and the Free World. Eastern Europe was dominated by Soviet communists.

Germany was divided into a communist East and a democratic West. Even the city of Berlin was split into communist and free zones.

Churchill called the military barrier around the Communist Bloc an Iron Curtain. The hostility between East and West was known as the Cold War, as the threat of nuclear destruction hung over the world.

The UN was essential for nations to work worldwide for peace, health, and education. Nothing could bring back the 72 million military personnel and civilians who died in World War II. The UN, however, symbolized hope that such a tragedy would never happen again.

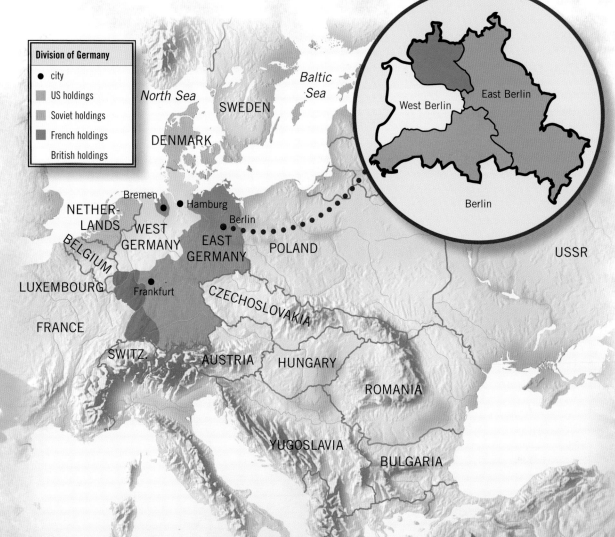

Division of Germany

- • city
- US holdings
- Soviet holdings
- French holdings
- British holdings

North Sea

Baltic Sea

SWEDEN

DENMARK

West Berlin

East Berlin

Berlin

NETHER-LANDS

Bremen

Hamburg

Berlin

POLAND

USSR

BELGIUM

WEST GERMANY

EAST GERMANY

LUXEMBOURG

Frankfurt

CZECHOSLOVAKIA

FRANCE

SWITZ.

AUSTRIA

HUNGARY

ROMANIA

YUGOSLAVIA

BULGARIA

Postwar Germany was divided into sectors by the Allies, as was the capital city of Berlin.

Nothing better symbolized the Cold War between the United States and the Soviet Union than the Berlin Wall, which divided East and West Germany and served as a barrier between communist Eastern Europe and the democratic West.

THE MARSHALL PLAN

EXHAUSTED FROM YEARS of war and suffering, most of the world gazed in shock at destroyed cities, shattered transportation systems, and ruined economies. Of the major combatants, only the continental United States had escaped enemy bombing. It was the United States that laid the framework for rebuilding Europe.

Led by former general and now secretary of state, George C. Marshall (1880–1959), the US government established a vast program to fund European recovery. Beginning in 1948, this Marshall Plan distributed $12 billion in economic aid to seventeen European nations, including West Germany.

A similar aid plan was extended to underdeveloped countries in 1949.

WAR DATA

Nations with the most deaths in World War II
(Combined military and civilian)

Soviet Union	23.1 million	United States	418,000
China	20 million	Korea	378,000
Germany	7.3 million	Lithuania	353,000
Poland	5.6 million	Czechoslovakia	345,000
Indonesia	4 million	Greece	311,000
Japan	2.7 million	Burma	272,000
Indian Empire	1.6 million	Netherlands	231,000
Indochina	1 million	Latvia	227,000
Yugoslavia	1 million	Philippines	147,000
Romania	833,000	Austria	105,000
Hungary	580,000	Ethiopia	100,000
France	567,000	Malaya	100,000
Italy	454,000	Finland	97,000
United Kingdom	450,000	Belgium	86,000

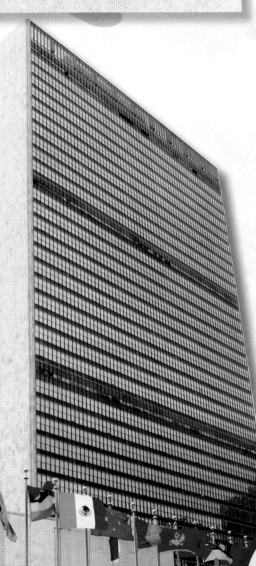

The United Nations building stands on New York City's East Side on what is recognized as "international territory."

Find Out More

WORDS TO KNOW

ace. A fighter pilot with many victories.

air power. The use of aircraft in war.

air support. Warplanes aiding ground forces.

aircraft carrier. Warships with aircraft and landing decks.

airlifted. Carried by aircraft to another area.

amphibious landing. Troops brought to a shore by vessels.

anti-aircraft guns. Artillery designed for firing at enemy aircraft.

antitank guns. Ground troops cannon for fighting armor.

armor. Thick-shelled vehicles armed with cannon and usually propelled by tracks, especially tanks.

artillery. Cannon, ranging from light field guns to heavy fortress artillery.

artillery barrage. Targeted firing by artillery.

atomic bomb. Nuclear-fission explosives.

barracks. Living quarters for troops.

battlefront. Area between two opposing forces.

battleship. Largest and most heavily armed warship.

bazookas. Shoulder-fired weapon for attacking armor.

beachhead. Area on an enemy shore captured by invading troops.

behind the lines. Area back from front lines for support troops, supplies, headquarters, and medical operations.

blackout. Keeping all lights out to prevent enemy forces from locating targets at night.

blitzkrieg. A "lightning war," one that breaks through enemy positions and surrounds them from the rear.

blockhouses. Fortified gun positions.

bombardment. Targeted bombing from the air or by artillery.

bunkers. Fortified chambers, usually underground.

campaign. Military operations in a specific region.

civil war. Conflict between forces from the same country.

co-belligerent. An ally who is not at war against every enemy of the alliance.

cold war. A state of hostility without military conflict.

combat medic. Infantry first-aid specialists in the field.

concentration camps. Prisons for holding large numbers of political prisoners.

convoys. Groups of merchant ships protected by warships.

counterattack. An offensive that follows an enemy attack.

counteroffensive. Large-scale counterattack.

cruiser. A medium-size warship.

czar. Russian emperor.

deploy. To send troops into a war zone.

deportation. To forcibly remove civilians from their homes.

destroyer. Warship smaller than a cruiser.

dictator. An absolute ruler more powerful than the government bureaucracy or legislature.

dive-bomber. Warplane designed to descend swiftly on a target and drop explosives.

draft. Required service in the military.

Fascism. A totalitarian system of government that asserts the right of the nation to dominate other nations.

field hospital. Medical facility near the battlefront.

fighter. Small, fast aircraft designed for attacking enemy troops, warplanes, and shipping.

forced labor. The use of prisoners to work for their captors.

gliders. Small aircraft without engines, pulled aloft by other planes that release them near the objective.

grenade. Hand-held explosive thrown by infantry.

hedgerow. a thick growth of trees or hedges bordering or separating fields.

Holocaust. Term for the Nazi persecution and murder of Jews and other people; a firestorm.

home front. The communities of a nation at war while its ground forces are campaigning in foreign lands.

hospital ships. Seagoing facilities for the seriously wounded.

incendiary bombs. Explosives designed to start fires.

"island-hopping." Allied strategy of bypassing enemy-held islands and leaving them to wither, unsupported.

Iron Curtain. A symbolic term for the closing off of communist countries after World War II.

kamikaze. Japanese pilots who intentionally crashed their warplanes into enemy targets.

landing craft. Small vessels specially designed for running up on beaches and landing troops and equipment.

long-range bombers. Aircraft capable of flying long distances at great heights and delivering large tonnages of bombs.

Luftwaffe. The German air force.

machine gun. A rapid-firing weapon used by all branches of the service.

marines. Troops trained to operate with naval units.

merchant ship. Civilian vessel carrying freight.

military tribunal. A court of military officers who are judges, defenders, and prosecutors; governed by international rules of war.

mine, minefields. Explosives hidden

underground, singly on trails or spread out by the hundreds in a field formation; designed to kill soldiers or destroy equipment, or, when placed under water, to destroy vessels.

mortar. A short-range rocket-launcher.

nationalism. The belief that one's country or nation is better than all others.

naval guns. Large-scale artillery on warships and often for shore fortifications.

nuclear war. War using atomic, or similar, bombs.

panzers. German term for armored vehicles.

paratroopers. Infantry trained to parachute into action from aircraft.

partisans (guerrillas). Fighters, usually civilians, operating in territory occupied by the enemy.

patrol boats. Fast, small craft that cruise near shore or up rivers, often on patrol and looking for the enemy.

pincers movement. A battle maneuver in which one side sends forces simultaneously around the left and right of an enemy, attempting to reunite these forces behind the enemy.

political prisoners. Civilians arrested for their political beliefs, usually with no right to a fair trial or lawyer.

puppet government. A government pretending to be answerable to its people, but actually under the control of a foreign power.

radar. An electronic warning system that detects the approach of aircraft; sonar is a system for underwater use.

refugees. Civilians forced from their homes by hostile actions.

resistance groups. Secret networks cooperating to fight or injure an occupying force.

"scorched earth" policy. The destruction, by a retreating army, of all crops, supplies, housing, and infrastructure that would be of use to an approaching invader.

seaplanes. Aircraft designed to land and take off on water siege. The surrounding of an enemy position or city, attempting to starve out the defenders or weaken their will to resist.

squadron. A small force under unified command: usually cavalry, aircraft, and warships.

submarine. Warship that operates under water; Germans termed it an *Unterzee Boot*, "undersea boat," or U-boat.

strategic bombing. Aerial bombardment that covers a vast area regardless of the risk to civilians.

strike force. A military unit organized to cause a powerful blow.

task force. A military force under one leader, with a temporary objective or purpose.

torpedo. A self-propelled, explosive-bearing projectile, launched from a vessel or aircraft, which can tear open the hull of a vessel and sink it.

totalitarianism. Absolute rule that forbids the ruled their civil and human rights.

trenches. Long, narrow ditches where troops take positions to block an enemy attack.

troop carriers. Motorized vehicles, often armored and tracked, for transporting infantry in a war zone.

truce. A temporary, agreed-upon lull in hostilities.

war reparations. The penalty defeated nations must pay to aid in reconstruction of the homelands of the victors.

wolf packs. Units of several German U-boats searching for merchant shipping to attack and sink.

FOR FURTHER READING

Adams, Simon. *World War II.* London and New York: DK Publishing in Association with the Imperial War Museum, 2000.

Churchill, Winston S., and the editors of *Life. The Second World War, Special Edition for Young Readers.* New York: Golden Press, 1960.

Hart, B.H. Liddell. *History of the Second World War.* Cambridge, Mass.: Da Capo Press, 1999

Murray, Aaron R., ed. *World War II Battles and Leaders.* London and New York: DK Publishing, 2004.

WEB SITES

BBC History - World War 2

www.bbc.co.uk/history/worldwars/wwtwo

History on the Net: World War Two

http://www.historyonthenet.com/WW2/bibliography.htm

The History Place

http://www.historyplace.com/worldwar2

Library of Congress

http://memory.loc.gov/learn/features/timeline/depwwii/wwarii/wwarii.html

National Archives Learning Curve

http://www.learningcurve.gov.uk/worldwar2/default.htm

123Explore!

http://www.123exp-history.com/t/03764853831/

OnWar.com; World War II Chronology

http://www.onwar.com/chrono/index.htm

Index

Credits

Abbreviations Used

JI = *Jupiter Images*; LoC = *Library of Congress*;
NARA = *National Archives and Records Administration*;
PD = *Public Domain*; SS = *Shutterstock*;
Wi = *Wikimedia*

l = left, *r* = right, *t* = top, *b* = bottom

3 NARA **4** NARA **6** LoC/Ezra C. Stiles **7***tl* JI **7**bl NARA
7*tr* Wi/*New York Times* **8***l* JI **8***r* Wi/PD **9***l* Wi/PD **9***tr* JI
9*br* JI **10**l JI **10***r* Wi/PD **11***l* JI **11***r* JI **12** JI **13** JI **14** JI
15 NARA **17***l* Wi/PD **17***r* JI **17***b* SS/Stephen Mulcahey
18 NARA **19***tl* NARA **19***tr* JI **19***br* Wi/PD **19***bl* JI
20 JI **21** NARA **22***l* NARA **22***r* Wi/PD **23***t* JI **23***b* Wi/PD
24*l* Wi/PD **24***r* Wi/PD **25** JI **26***tl* LoC **26***tr* NARA
26*bl* JI **27***l* NARA **27***r* NARA **28***l* Wi/PD **28***r* Wi/PD

29*t* JI **29***b* JI **30***l* LoC **30***r* JI **31** NARA **33***l* Wi/PD
33*tr* Wi/PD **33***br* JI **34***l* JI **34***r* Wi/PD **35** NARA
36*l* Wi/PD **36***r* JI **37** JI **38** SS/fengshui **39***t* JI
39*b* SS/Richard A. McGuirk **40***l* JI **40***r* JI **41***l* LoC
41*r* JI **42***tr* NARA **42***br* Wi/PD **43** Wi/PD **44** Wi/PD
45 SS/photogl **47** Wi/PD **48** NARA **49** JI **50** JI
51 Wi/PD **53** NARA **54** Wi **55** Wi/*Oeuvre personnelle*
56 NARA **57***l* NARA **57***r* Wi/PD **58** NARA **59***t* Wi/PD
59*b* Wi/PD **60***bl* Wi/PD **60***tr* NARA **61** NARA
62 NARA **63***t* Wi/PD **63***b* JI **64***l* NARA **64***r* NARA
65*t* NARA **65***b* Wi/PD **67***t* JI **67***b* SS/Steve Broer

Backgrounds JI; SS/Charles Taylor

Cover NARA; SS/0037729165; SS/Tony Campbell;
SS/Scott Rothstein; JI; SS/Doug Matthews